Just Watch the Game

Just Watch The Game

John Steigerwald

Published by
Little M Productions
119 Fairway Landings Dr.
Canonsburg, PA 15317

Paperback ISBN: 978-0-578-07446-7
Hardcover ISBN: 978-0-578-06811-4

Printed in the United States of America

Contents

This book is dedicated to Emma, Katie, Gunnar, Luke, Jake and Wyatt.

One day, during the Summer of '91, I walked into my parent's home in Scott Township, the house where I grew up, and sitting on the dining room table, with no one around, was the Stanley Cup. My brother Paul had been given custody of the Cup for a day. I think of that and this picture of my dad every time I see the Cup being wheeled out for the presentation to the new champion.

FOREWORD

PICTURE a warm summer night at Forbes Field in Pittsburgh in the mid-'50s. There are 10,000 to 15,000 fans there to watch a bad Pirates team and my dad and I are among them.

I'm seven or eight years old and thrilled to be there, but I'm a little distracted by the popcorn vendor a section or two away. I'm in the early stages of a lifetime popcorn addiction and I'm trying to decide whether to ask my dad for popcorn now or go for the ice cream later. It was an either-or situation. I had no chance of getting both. As I'm watching the popcorn guy and trying to decide if it's a good time to bother my dad for some money, I feel a slight nudge. I turn toward my dad and he gives me an impatient look, nods toward the field and says, "Just watch the game."

I didn't bother telling him that I had decided it was time to eat and that I had decided on popcorn because I knew what the answer would be.

"We didn't come here to eat."

Fifty years later and what do we have? We have the Pirates offering "All You Can Eat" tickets. Every night, PNC Park is filled with people who would have answered my dad by saying, "Yes we did." But that's another story and we'll get to that later in the book.

I loved going to Pirates games so much when I was a kid that, if I had been told I was not allowed to eat or drink anything, it wouldn't have made a difference. In all my years as a fan and in the more than 30 years of covering sports as a journalist, all I've ever really wanted to do is watch the game. Blame my dad for that.

You can blame my dad for this book, too. If not for him I would never have developed the interest in sports that would have driven me to try to find work in such a competitive business.

When you're 61 years old, as I am, it's not easy to search the recesses of your mind and come up with your earliest memory.

If I had to pick out a single incident, I'd probably have to go with the first day of kindergarten, which would have been when I was a month shy of my fifth birthday. I remember that well, but my earliest memory isn't of a single event, it's a general recollection of being put to bed by my dad while listening to sports on the radio.

In my mind's eye I can see that it's still light outside, there's a radio on the table next to my bed, my dad is hovering over me and I can hear the voice of Joe Tucker, longtime WWSW radio announcer and former Voice of the Steelers, reading the race results.

I'm guessing I was three or four years old.

Some kids got bedtime stories and lullabies. I got Joe Tucker and horseracing results. I don't remember having any trouble falling asleep.

Later on, I would watch my dad watch the Pirates on TV while he was listening to a Steelers exhibition game on the radio and it seemed like a perfectly sensible thing to do. My dad, Bill Steigerwald, known to his friends as "Stag," was obviously a huge influence in my life. Because of him, I grew up surrounded by sports.

Something else I was surrounded by: opinions.

I'm known as an opinionated guy. My dad's opinion of me would be that I'm not opinionated enough. He was actually of the opinion that people who weren't opinionated were boring. I tend to agree with that opinion. What would sports be without arguments? And you can't have arguments without opinions.

Of course, that's just my opinion.

My friends in the media would tell me about running into my dad and they would say, "Now I know where you get all of your ideas."

I didn't get ideas from my dad as much as I got a general philosophy of life.

- Skeptical bordering on cynical.
- Always question the conventional wisdom.
- Never follow the crowd.
- If everybody in school is wearing black shoes, you wear brown.

I remember in 1972 when there was a lot of talk about the Steelers drafting a running back. Lydell Mitchell of Penn State was generally accepted as one of the best backs in the country. My dad said to me, "I'll tell you who I would draft ahead of Mitchell —Franco Harris. He's a perfect NFL back and I think he's the better of the two."

When everybody in Pittsburgh was looking at Terry Hanratty, the quarterback from Butler and Notre Dame, as the Steelers savior, my dad said, "Overrated. The Notre Dame fans are out of their minds." He was right.

When I started covering sports for a living, I made a habit of questioning the conventional wisdom and I think it paid off for me.

My mother, Kay, who, at this writing is 92 years old, is still one of the smartest people I know. She's still quick enough to win a "Jeopardy!" championship and she taught me as much about vocabulary, grammar and good writing as any teacher I ever had.

When my brothers Bill and Paul suggested that I write a book, at first I dismissed the idea. Then I started thinking about all the things I had seen and the people I had met over the last 38 years and I thought that it might be fun. As I started thinking about what subjects to cover, I came to the realization that I was a pretty lucky guy. I covered three Super Bowl winners, a World Series winner, Three Stanley Cup winners and a heavyweight boxing champion. As you will read later, I also think that I covered the man who did the greatest job of coaching in the history of North American professional sports, the greatest hockey player who ever lived and the best NFL team of all time.

As a fan, I was there for the most famous play in NFL history and I'm old enough to have vivid memories of the best World Series ever played and the greatest home run ever hit. I saw the first and last baseball games played at Three Rivers Stadium. I saw the first hockey game played at what was then the Civic Arena.

That's a lot to write about.

Riding the buses in baseball's minor leagues also provided a lot of material for this book, including my pleasant and not-so pleasant encounters with some of baseball's immortals.

My TV career began in 1978 when local stations were still shooting stories on film and ended when they were shooting stories with digital cameras that had no film or tape. I saw local news go from something to be proud of to something bordering on a pathetic joke. I worked with two broadcasting legends, Myron Cope and my idol, Bob Prince. I was part of the Steelers traveling party for close to 20 years including trips to Spain, Ireland and Japan.

And then there are opinions. I still have plenty of those and there is no shortage of them in these pages. You might even find some of them offensive. I sure hope so.

CHAPTER 1

ULTIMATE GRAND SLAMS

IT'S Wednesday night, July 25th, 1956. I'm about two months shy of my eighth birthday and I'm with my dad, sitting behind home plate at Forbes Field. There are only a few thousand people left because it's the bottom of the ninth and the Pirates are behind the Cubs, 8-5. The Pirates were a bad team at 42-46 but the Cubs were worse. They were 39-47. My dad and I didn't know it but we were about to witness something that had never happened in the history of Major League Baseball. And after it happened we had no idea that, 54 years later, it would not have been done again.

Bob Friend took a four nothing lead into the eighth inning and gave up four runs before he could get the second out. Elroy Face came in and gave up three more runs in the eighth to make it 7-4. The Pirates cut it to 7-5 with a run in their half of the eighth and Face gave up another run in the top of the ninth.

So, it's 8-5 Cubs and it's looking very much like the Pirates have blown a big lead to a bad team and are about to lose. My dad and I are behind home plate because we're following my dad's usual strategy of leaving his regular upper deck, third-base box seat and finding an empty seat near an exit on the lower level so we can beat the traffic. When you were behind home plate at Forbes Field, you were right on top of the action and this was a perfect time to be behind home plate.

The Pirates loaded the bases with no outs against Jim Brosnan, one of the best relief pitchers in the league. Roberto Clemente, 21 years old and in his second Major League season, is the hitter. I would be lying if I told you I remember where Clemente's hit went. But I can still see him flying around second base with his arms flailing as clearly as if I had seen it last night. I can still see him headed for third, arms still flailing and showing no intention of stopping. I can still see Bobby Bragan, the third base coach, who also was the manager, holding his arms above his head giving a very emphatic STOP sign. And now I can still see Clemente blowing by Bragan and heading down the third base line right at me. The ball and Clemente come to the plate at the same time. The Cubs catcher, Hobey Landrith, tries to make the tag. I can see the home plate umpire, Bill Engein, giving the safe sign and Landrith immediately and violently jumping up to get in Engein's face to dispute the call. And I can feel my dad taking me by the arm and pulling me toward the exit and I can hear him saying, "Let's go."

Seeing something that had never happened in baseball history didn't change the fact that we had to beat the traffic.

Clemente hit what is now known as an Ultimate Grand Slam — a walk-off grand slam home run that wins a game by one run. Your team has to be behind by three and it has to be the bottom of the ninth. Up until July 25, 1956 it had only been done eight times since records were kept beginning in 1881.

But Clemente's was an *inside the park* Ultimate Grand Slam and that had never been done before and, as of this writing, it hasn't been done since.

That is my second earliest sports memory and I can honestly say I've never witnessed a more exciting moment in a game. So I guess that means it's been pretty much downhill after that.

And now I know you're on the edge of your seat wondering what my earliest sports memory is.

It's 2½ months earlier in the same year, May 11, 1956. The Pirates are behind the Phillies 5-2. It's the bottom of the ninth and Danny Kravitz, a journeyman catcher, is the Pirates' hitter. Jack Meyer is pitching for the Phillies. My dad was not one of those guys who made a lot of noise at games. If someone would hit a home run, he'd give a little fist pump and that would be it. Every once in a while he would blurt something out that was only loud enough for the people in his section to hear. I remember that night hearing him say, "C'mon, Kravitz. Hit one in the seats."

Remember, I'm 7½.

I still had my popcorn container, which, in what was then an example of marketing genius, was in the shape of a megaphone. I put it to my lips and I yelled. "Come on, Kravitz. Hit one in the seats."

Next pitch: Bang, in the right field seats. Ultimate Grand Slam. Pirates win, 6-5. Of course I was convinced that I had done a better job than my dad because I was sure that my decision to use the megaphone meant that Kravitz actually heard me and followed my instructions.

Danny Kravitz was my favorite player for quite a while after that. I don't remember if I switched to Clemente after he topped Kravitz two months later but I have a feeling I didn't because I was sure that I had actually *caused* him to hit his.

Kravitz was the eighth player in history to hit an Ultimate Grand Slam and two months later Clemente became the ninth and I was there to see them both. Amazing. Maybe that's why going to the game was always enough for me. Maybe I went expecting to see drama like that every night. Nobody had to promise me any fireworks or a bobblehead. I was happy to be there to "Just Watch the Game" and wait for a memory.

Here's something else about Clemente's UGS. I remember reading about it in the paper the next day and I remember reading or hearing — maybe both — quite a bit of discussion about whether Clemente should have been fined for running through the stop sign at third base. (He wasn't.) I was 7½ and I distinctly remember doing what I did every day, which was spreading the Post-Gazette sports page out on the floor and lying there reading about the previous night's game that had almost always ended before my bed time.

Do you know any second graders who read the sports page today? I know I wasn't the only one doing it back then.

Nineteen years later, I got a first-hand account of what happened that night from the man who put up the stop sign. Bobby Bragan, who was then the president of the Texas League, joined me in the Lafayette Drillers radio booth and he assured me that it happened exactly the way I remembered it.

A few years ago I asked my dad if he remembered being at Forbes Field that night and he said, "Not really."

The fact that my brother, Dan, was born the next day might have had something to do with that.

CHAPTER 2

SHORT STOP
PASSING ON THE GOOSE EGGS

I T was August 14, 1971, and the Pirates, who had been struggling for a while and had seen their lead over the second-place Cardinals reduced to four games, were playing the Cardinals at Three Rivers Stadium.

Bob Gibson was pitching for St. Louis.

My buddy Goose and I did what we did 60 or 70 times that season. We lied and said we were 18, bought two $2 general admission tickets, bribed "Hooks" the usher and sat in box seats along the third base line.

It was obvious right away that Gibson was going to be tough. The Pirates weren't just going three up and three down. They seemed to be doing it in about a minute and a half per inning. Meanwhile, the Cardinals were bashing the Pirates pitchers all over the lot. Bob Johnson gave up five runs in the first and was taken out before he could get the second out.

It was a Saturday afternoon and there were over 30,000 people there — a huge crowd for the Pirates. By the fifth inning it was obvious that the Pirates were going to have a tough time getting a loud fall ball off of Gibson much less a hit.

Goose and I decided that if somebody was going to pitch a no-hitter against the Pirates, we sure as hell weren't going to be there to see it. We had no interest in hearing 30,000 people cheer for a Pirates loss.

I guess being a fan was a little different then. At least it was for the crowd I ran with. We weren't wearing Pirates jerseys — in fact, we wouldn't be caught dead in one — but we considered the visiting team the enemy.

After Gibson retired the side in the seventh, Goose and I got up and headed for the exit. As the people in our row we're getting up to let us pass, they were saying, "Hey, where are you guys going? He's got a no-hitter going."

We said, "Yeah, we know. That's why we're leaving."

They looked at us like we were nuts. Goose and I couldn't understand why anybody would want to see the Pirates lose.

We were driving up the Green Tree hill on the Parkway West listening to the radio when we heard the crowd cheer after Bob Prince described Gibson's strikeout of Willie Stargell for the 27th out. To this day, we're still convinced that we did the right thing.

CHAPTER 3

THE GAME EXPERIENCE

JERRY Jones, the owner of the Dallas Cowboys, was able to finagle $1.1 billion out of his local government for a new stadium and a good bit of that money was used to pay for a video screen that stretches from 20-yard-line to 20- yard-line. In the 2009 preseason there was a little bit of a problem when a punt clanged off the bottom of it.

Do over.

Yep. Just like we used to do when a pass hit the telephone wire when we were playing touch football in the street. Jerry didn't have a problem with it and the NFL didn't have enough of a problem to force Jones to raise it a few feet or, better yet, blow it up.

We can only hope that, some day soon, the Cowboys have a blocked do-over punt cost them a trip to the Super Bowl.

Jerry said he wanted the video screen to be that big because he wanted Cowboys fans to have the best "Game Experience" in the NFL.

Game experience.

Now there's an expression that should make any real sports fan want to vomit.

I liked it better when the game *was* the experience.

There's no way any young Cowboys fan is going to get more excited about walking into the new stadium and seeing the Video Monstrosity than I did when I walked into Forbes Field in the '50s and '60s and saw the green grass and the perfectly manicured infield.

That was enough. The game was gravy. Just being there was enough of an experience for a kid back then. If you went to Forbes Field to see the Pirates or the Steelers, or to Pitt Stadium to see Pitt or the Steelers, there's no question that you were there to *just watch the game.*

FORBES FIELD

I never had a problem with Forbes Field and would have been happy if it had been allowed to become a shrine like Wrigley Field and Fenway Park. And, by the way, I've been to both of those shrines and neither is as nice as Forbes Field was. Forbes Field had all the "charm" of the other two if bad sightlines, no legroom and seats too small for Christina Aguilera's ass qualify as charm, but it had something that neither of the other two have.

Wide open spaces.

Here are the outfield dimensions of Forbes Field from the leftfield line to the rightfield line:

LF 365 (with a 35-foot high scoreboard)
LC 406 (the wall was 12-feet high all the way around).
CF 457
RC 436
RRC 375
RF 300 (with a 27-foot high screen)

That was a lot of bright green grass in the middle of all that concrete and red brick in Oakland.

One of the little quirks I never thought about until recently is how home runs used to disappear at night. From the 375-mark in right center-field to the leftfield line, there were no stands behind the wall. Just Schenley Park. At night, that white ball was easy to follow against the black sky as it headed toward the wall and then, when it passed under the lights, poof, it just disappeared.

A home run really was going, going and then literally gone.

It was a lot more dramatic than, say, seeing one bounce off that big vacuum cleaner that they used to park behind the center field fence at Three Rivers Stadium.

My favorite spot at Forbes Field was at the very end of the right field stands, just above the 375 mark. We would buy general admission tickets and stand in the aisle, right next to the exit gate. The warning track was just 12 feet below us.

I was a huge Roberto Clemente fan and my favorite non-Pirate was Willie Mays. That was a great spot when the Giants were in town.

I remember an August doubleheader with the Giants in 1960. I was not quite 12 and had taken a bus and streetcar to the game from the South Hills with no adult supervision. We somehow managed to get to the game without being kidnapped and/or murdered.

Early in the first game, a kid, who wasn't in our group, had dropped his sunglasses on the warning track below us. We kept yelling at the Pirates centerfielder, Bill Virdon, and Mays to come over and pick them up. Virdon never acknowledged us but Mays, with his back to us, kept giving us a wave trying to get us to shut up. I'll bet every kid who was there that day remembers the time Willie Mays actually acknowledged his existence.

At the end of the first game, Virdon came over, picked up the sunglasses and threw them up to the kid. That was probably the biggest thrill of that kid's life. You wonder sometimes if players know how easy it is to have a major impact on young fans.

Somewhere there's a guy in his 60s who still remembers the day Bill Virdon retrieved his sunglasses. I hope he's reading this.

Two other things I remember about that day: Gino Cimoli, who played right field in the first game and center field in the second, hit two triples to the same spot — right below us at the 375 mark. On one of them I could have almost reached down and stolen Mays' hat.

The game was on national TV and the presidential election was only about two-and-a-half months away. Early in game one, a guy came down the aisle with a "JFK for President" banner and paid a kid 50 cents (good for a hot dog and a Coke and maybe an ice cream in those days) to hang it over the railing above the 375 mark.

That lasted about half an inning before an usher came by and grabbed it. Or maybe it was Haldeman or Ehrlichman disguised as an usher.

We stayed for the doubleheader, caught the streetcar and the bus and made it home to Scott Township alive. That was a game experience Jerry Jones would never understand.

***

As a football stadium, Forbes Field was a really nice baseball park. It just wasn't designed for watching football. Too many of the seats were too close to the ground and they used temporary bleachers that ran from the leftfield foul line into right centerfield. You knew that anybody who was there for a Steelers game was there to *just watch the game*. The lack of amenities and all the inconveniences meant that the stands were filled mostly with men for whom the game was the attraction because there was no other attraction. My dad had a season ticket to Steelers games beginning in 1946. Notice I said "ticket" not "tickets."

One ticket.

Going to a Steelers game wasn't a social event. It was a sporting event. A game.

I got to go to a lot of games on my uncle Jack's ticket. My dad's brother was in the CIA and lived all over the world from London to Singapore and Tokyo, but he was a huge sports fan and kept his Steelers season ticket. Again —ticket, not tickets. It was one aisle in back of my dad's seat and about 10 seats to his right. I would ride to the game with my dad and sit in Uncle Jack's seat by myself.

I started doing it when I was about 10 years old.

And you wonder why my attitude has always been *just watch the game*? I can remember how small and alone I felt being squished between two giant adult men for 2½ hours (that's how long games were back then), enveloped in cigarette and cigar smoke, with nobody to talk to and loving every minute of it.

PITT STADIUM

Pitt Stadium was a better place to watch football than Forbes Field if you didn't mind pulling splinters out of your ass. There really wasn't a bad seat in the house as long as you're talking about the sightlines and not the actual seats because there were no seats.

Just benches.

For most of the life of the stadium, the benches were made out of wood, although they did eventually change them to aluminum. That eliminated the splinters but made for some cold buns in November and December.

When the Steelers played there in the '60s, they had terrible teams and that meant lots of empty seats. If you were under 18, you could sit in the end zone for $1 and, still, there would be 20,000 empty seats.

But, you know what?

Every person in the stadium was there for one reason and one reason only.

To *just watch the game.*

The game experience consisted of sitting your butt on the bench and watching the Steelers and/or Pitt figure out a way to lose.

Most of the Pitt teams in the '60s also stunk.

There was no tailgating because there were no parking lots. Everybody had their favorite gas station on Forbes Avenue or driveway on an Oakland side street. That was part of the adventure – finding a parking place. Walking through Oakland and up Cardiac Hill to the stadium was also part of the game experience. You were only willing to experience it if your Number One purpose for being there was to *just watch the game.*

I remember going to a few Steelers games with my friend, Bill Scattaregia and his dad. Mr. Scat and his 60-something buddies had a system that included meeting at a parking lot and arranging for a van to take them up Cardiac Hill. I remember lots of cigar smoke. They weren't wearing Steelers jerseys and there were no wives. They didn't see a need to set up a grill and cook a meal before heading to the game. Keep in mind that these guys did this so that they could watch a pathetically bad football team lose almost every Sunday.

Pitt Stadium was never completed. At least, it looked like construction had been stopped for lack of funds. When you came through the gate you saw mounds of dirt and exposed steel beams.

No restaurants.

No gift shops.

No luxury suites.

Just, concrete, steel, dirt and the beautiful smell of an old stadium mixed with hot chocolate, coffee, popcorn, hot dogs and cigarette and cigar smoke. You knew that you were not at a social event. You knew that there was only one reason for every person you saw to be there.

To *just watch the game.*

Because there was no tailgating and because you wanted to minimize the amount of time that you exposed your butt cheeks to those icy benches, the objective was to be walking into the stadium just as PA announcer Ray Downey was belting out the starting lineups. Your hope was to time it perfectly so that your butt was hitting the bench at the exact moment the kicker's foot was hitting the ball.

My dad had it down to a science. He would drive me and my friends to the games, we would buy our $1 end-zone tickets and he would sit in his reserved seat on the 40-yard line. We rarely got there more than five minutes before kickoff and his instructions were to get to the car immediately after the game so that we could beat the traffic.

We liked that plan because it gave us a chance to get home and play some football in the street before dark.

Again, no tailgating.

How many of the 65,000 who show up at Heinz Field for Steelers games would continue to show up if Heinz Field were magically changed into Pitt Stadium?

I'm guessing less than half.

You can eliminate at least half of the women immediately. You can also eliminate half of the men who wouldn't be able to comprehend the idea of not drinking beer for three hours in the parking lot before the game. Eliminate 90 per cent of the people in the luxury suites.

I think you'd be left with 25,000 fans — tops.

But, I also think that the Steelers could find 40,000 new customers, who wanted to *just watch the game,* in about 20 minutes.

THREE RIVERS STADIUM

From about 1979 on, Three Rivers Stadium was a dump. Oh, it was fine for the Steelers, but it was one of the worst things that ever happened to the Pirates. Of course, so was PNC Park, but for opposite reasons. More on that in a minute.

I was there for the first Pirates game at Three Rivers Stadium in June of 1970 and I admit I was like everybody else. I was in shock. I couldn't believe how beautiful it was. The comfortable seats. The electronic scoreboard.

The artificial turf. I even liked the Pirates' double-knit uniforms, the first buttonless, form-fitting baseball uniforms in the history of the planet.

The experience bordered on the surreal, really.

It felt like a giant leap into the future because it was so unlike any stadium I had ever been in before.

Then, some time in the summer of 1974, I changed my mind. I realized that Three Rivers Stadium and all the other cookie-cutter stadiums that had popped up were hideous baseball venues.

It was my first year of doing radio play-by-play in the minor leagues and I had been re-introduced to ballparks that had been built, in most cases, many, many years before, for baseball only. I realized how much more interesting baseball was when it was played in a ballpark that had it's own idiosyncrasies.

The minor league parks not only had character. They each had their own character. Lawrence Stadium in Wichita, where the team I worked for played, had a deep centerfield fence with a huge, green hitter's background that was in play. The park in Evansville had railroad tracks running directly behind the right field fence.

The dimensions were different in every park. And they all had grass. Real grass. And no sliding pits around the bases. Remember sliding pits? How ugly were they?

I worked in three different minor leagues from 1974 to 1976 and had spent time in more than 20 unique ballparks, so when I came back to Pittsburgh at the end of those minor league seasons and went to Three Rivers Stadium I was stunned by how ugly it was.

When I started working in Pittsburgh and began to refer to Three Rivers as a dump, many of the fine citizens of Western Pennsylvania were offended and let me know it with their friendly cards and letters.

Most of my friends in the media disagreed with me.

It was another case of me being right and just about everybody else being wrong. I never changed my opinion. It took 20 years before the Buffalo Bisons of the International League showed everybody in baseball the way to go. They built a new ballpark, but they went out of their way to make it look like an old one. It was a huge hit and they started selling out every game.

The Orioles were the first Major League team to follow the Bisons' lead and now almost every team in Major League Baseball plays in a ball-park that was built for baseball only and is a throwback to the parks that were built 100 years ago.

Remember in 1991 when Pittsburgh Mayor Sophie Masloff came out and said that the Pirates should build a new "intimate" ballpark for 45,000 patterned after Forbes Field and call it Roberto Clemente Stadium?

Everybody laughed at her.

The first sentence in my Post-Gazette column the following Saturday went like this: "Sophie Masloff for President."

I knew she was right.

Three Rivers was killing the Pirates for all kinds of reasons, but mostly because it was too big. There was no urgency for the fans to buy tickets. They could wait until they saw how the team was doing or what the weather was before they made the decision to go to a game. Anybody who knows anything about selling baseball tickets knows that it's all about the advance sales. If you depend on walkup sales you get what the Pirates got for most of the '70s and '80s.

Depressingly small crowds — which leads to more depressingly small crowds.

I can remember some of my media friends laughing at me when I told them that the Pirates should build a ballpark that seats no more than 35,000. Of course, that's what they did in 2001 with PNC Park.

The traffic before and after games at Three Rivers was a nightmare and the atmosphere inside the stadium was depressing. Imagine how bad the attendance would have been if they hadn't had one of the best teams in baseball for 10 years.

The radio and TV ratings showed that the fans were still out there and the attendance showed that they hated the stadium. So, for about 23 years, I took every opportunity to refer to Three Rivers Stadium as a dump and I was right.

Three Rivers almost killed the Pirates. Of course, the Pirates made up for having a hideous stadium that everybody hated by doing either no marketing at all or doing counter-productive marketing. And, of course, they fired their best marketing tool, Bob Prince.

When I would blame the Pirates' terrible attendance on Three Rivers Stadium, inevitably someone would point to the Reds, who were averaging over 40,000 per game at Riverfront Stadium, which was every bit as hideous as Three Rivers.

I would point out that the Reds had close to 10 million people to draw from within a 50- to 100-mile radius.

The Pirates had 2½ million.

The Reds had over 100 stations on their radio network.

The Pirates had 30.

The Reds overcame their stadium problem by taking advantage of their potential customer base.

The Pirates had no clue how to take full advantage of the small number of potential customers available to them and because of the unpopularity of the stadium, they should have been super-aggressive in their marketing approach.

Instead, they had no marketing approach.

There also was a vicious circle involved. The Reds filled their stadium with busloads of fans from as far away as Charleston, West Virginia, and that created an atmosphere that made people want to come back.

The Pirates put a good team on the field and thought that would do the trick. It created an atmosphere that made people wonder why they came.

I saw a perfect example of the difference between how the Pirates marketed the team and how the Reds marketed theirs every time a Pirates-Reds score was given over the PA system at Watt Powell Park in Charleston. If the Reds won, there would be a loud cheer. (Actually "loud" is stretching it since on most nights there were about 800 people in the park.) This despite the fact that most of the players on the Pirates' roster had played in Charleston with the Charlies.

I called the games for the Pirates Triple "A" affiliate on an FM station and the AM station owned by the same company carried the Reds' games. Several chartered buses would leave Charleston for Cincinnati every weekend that the Reds were home. The Pirates did no promotion or marketing in Charleston because the Pirates General Manager, Joe L. Brown, didn't want to hurt the Charlies' ticket sales.

In 1976, the year I worked in Charleston, the Charlies drew 72,000 for 70 home games and 8,000 of those showed up for two major promotions. How much could he have hurt ticket sales?

The distance between Charleston and Cincinnati is virtually the same as the distance between Charleston and Pittsburgh. But the Pirates, who had one-fourth the population to draw from that the Reds had, conceded the Charleston market to the Reds.

The Pirates didn't hire a real marketing director until 1980, the year after they won the World Series. His name was Jack Schrom and he was a really, really, nice guy. He also was a disaster for the Pirates.

Schrom decided that the way to boost the Pirates' attendance was to promote them as family entertainment. I think it was Jerry Seinfeld who said many years later, "There's no such thing as fun for the whole family."

Too bad he didn't tell Schrom that in 1980.

Pirates fans watching on TV were bombarded with promotions about the Pirate Parrot's birthday party. Disney characters were everywhere, including dancing on top of the dugouts in between innings. I remember one year when the Pirates' yearbook had the Pirate Parrot on the cover.

Intelligent people actually thought that there were enough parents out there who would be willing to buy four tickets to a Pirates game so that their kids could watch a guy in a parrot suit. It turned out the guy in the Parrot suit was really funny because he was high on cocaine most of the time, but that's another story.

Schrom had this vision of mom, dad and the two perfect looking kids, skipping through the turnstiles. Something you might see on a Kellogg's Corn Flakes box. I used to lean over from the press box to see how many families of four I could find and I don't remember ever finding one.

I ripped Schrom and made fun of his promotions at every opportunity. Eventually, he was fired or resigned and the Pirates started promoting baseball again. Attendance numbers didn't exactly explode but at least you could watch a game on TV without throwing up. If they had stuck with Schrom's approach attendance would have gotten even worse.

PNC PARK

I was there for the first game at PNC Park on March 31, 2001. It was a Sunday night exhibition game against the New York Mets. Here's what I said for my show-opening line on KDKA's "Sports Showdown" at 11:35 that night:

"PNC Park is the nicest ballpark I have ever seen in my life and is probably the nicest ballpark on the planet Earth and it's the worst thing that could have happened to Pirates fans."

I don't remember getting a lot of agreement from the other panelists that night but I knew it meant that the Pirates could get away with putting pathetic excuses for Major League Baseball teams on the field for several more years.

Guess what they would be selling from now on.

If you said "Game Experience," go to the head of the class.

As I write this, the Pirates have completed 10 seasons in PNC Park and everybody knows that Pirates baseball in the 21st century is all about the food, fireworks and bobble heads.

PNC Park has allowed the Pirates to become a Major League team in name only and still draw close to 20,000 fans per game. I began telling people in 2003 that, if they don't like the product they're getting from the Pirates they should stop buying tickets.

That did wonders for my hate mail and even got me a meeting with the KDKA news director who had gotten complaints from the Pirates front office.

It got me a lot of angry looks and quite a few angry comments when I had to go to PNC Park to do a live shot for the 6 o'clock news. I did my last live shot there in June of 2005 and my plan right now is to never set foot in PNC Park again.

I also plan to never take seriously the opinion of people who continue to buy a product they profess to despise.

So, let's review. I said PNC Park would be terrible for real Pirates fans — the ones who actually want to have a competitive baseball team. I was right and just about everybody else was wrong.

One last thought on "Game Experience." My friends and I probably bought tickets to 60 Pirates games a year from 1970 through 1972 and I can honestly tell you that, if the Pirates had announced in April of 1970 that they would no longer be selling food or beer at their games, it wouldn't have affected our attendance by a single game.

For us, it was enough to *just watch the game*.

CHAPTER 4

FREE FOOD AND EVERYTHING

I remember my first press pass.

It was the summer of 1971 and I was going to summer school at Kent State and doing afternoon sports reports for WKSU-FM, the campus radio station. Even though WKSU was a quasi-legitimate station that penetrated the Akron, Youngstown and Cleveland markets and actually had listeners because of its classical music and jazz format, when I called the PGA about getting press passes to the Firestone Classic at nearby Firestone Country Club for me and my fellow WKSU sports reporter, Larry Clisby, I fully expected whoever answered to laugh and then hang up on me.

I couldn't believe how nice the guy was.

He actually treated me like a real radio sportscaster and said he'd be glad to leave credentials for Larry and me at the press gate.

Larry (also known as "Big C," and the longtime voice of Purdue basketball) and I didn't know what to expect when we got to the golf tournament but we were stunned when we saw what was in our media packet. There was an official armband and press badge that gave us access inside the ropes and to the press tent. But it was the tickets for the free food that really let us know that we had arrived. There we were, two college kids, mingling and sitting down to dinner with the media stars — from the Youngstown, Akron and Cleveland sportscasters and writers to the biggest names in the national media.

I found out a few years later that nobody who covers a golf tournament actually goes out on the course. They watch the tournament on TV in the press tent and wait for the golfers to come in for their post-round interviews. It's air-conditioned and there's lots of free food. I wasn't about to hang out in a press tent. I put my WKSU tape recorder over my shoulder and headed out to watch some golf. I had never seen a PGA tour event in person and I was going to take advantage of my inside-the-rope access.

I also got a quick lesson in the power of the media when I ventured into the press tent for the first time. It was packed with reporters sitting in chairs in front of a podium. Jerry Heard, a relative unknown, was the leader after two rounds and he spoke first. Jack Nicklaus was the next speaker. Now, keep in mind that there was nobody in sports bigger than Jack Nicklaus at the time. I wasn't seated in the crowd. I was standing just a few feet away from the podium where I had placed my microphone with the WKSU flag on it. Nicklaus stepped up to the podium and a few seconds went by without a question being asked. So, I, the snot-nosed kid from the college radio station, filled the void by asking the first official question of my career.

SNOT NOSED COLLEGE KID: "Are you gonna catch him?"

GREATEST GOLFER ON EARTH: "He's gonna have to get a helluva lot of bogeys and I'm gonna have to get a helluva lot of birdies."

If you ever pay a visit to the Golf Hall of Fame, you probably shouldn't expect to find that exchange there.

Nicklaus went on with the press conference but I didn't hear a word he said. All I knew was that I had looked Jack Nicklaus in the eye and asked him a question and he answered it.

But it got even better.

The next day I was back on campus. I picked up a copy of the Sunday Cleveland Plain Dealer and went to the sports section. There was an Associated Press story about the Firestone Classic on the front page. The first sentence of the story was a quote:

"He's gonna have to get a helluva lot of bogeys and I'm gonna have to get a helluva lot of birdies."

That was Nicklaus' answer to my question! Right there in the Cleveland Plain Dealer.

Later that day, a friend of mine who had gone home to Columbus showed me a copy of the Columbus Dispatch. There was the AP story that started with the answer to my question again.

Then it dawned on me. That was the AP. That story went to newspapers all over the world. I was almost famous. Maybe that's why I was never shy about asking questions at press conferences. I also learned that sometimes innocuous or stupid questions can get useful answers, something athletes and coaches never seem to understand.

Two summers later I had another up-close-and-personal moment that made me a Jack Nicklaus fan for life. It was the U.S. Open at Oakmont. I was working for Color Channel 3, a local-access cable TV station in Sharon, Pa., and managed to get a press pass. I recruited my buddy Goose to be the cameraman, grabbed the station's dinky black-and-white porta-pack video camera and headed for Oakmont planning to bring back some big interviews and impress the boss.

Jack Nicklaus was an even bigger star in 1973 than he was in 1971 and I wanted to get my first big one-on-one interview with him. They did things a little differently back then. There were no TV cameras in the press tent so, after the golfers did a press conference with the writers, they would go outside and do a series of one-on-one interviews for television. The cameras were lined up next to each other with ABC first, followed by KDKA, WTAE and WIIC (now WPXI) not necessarily in that order, and then Color Channel 3. Remember, ABC and the three local Pittsburgh stations were still shooting their in-the-field interviews on film in those days. They all had their huge, impressive looking studio cameras lined up to shoot the interview on video tape. I had my dinky little black-and-white porta-pack.

I stood there with my little plastic microphone watching Nicklaus moving down the line, starting with Frank Gifford of ABC, followed by the local sportscasters, and I have to say I was feeling pretty self-conscious and pretty ridiculous.

And really, really nervous.

I fully expected Nicklaus, after having to answer the same questions four times from real, big-time sportscasters, to look at me with my pathetic little black-and-white camera and either laugh or walk away or both.

I introduced myself and shook his hand and he treated me *exactly* the same way he treated the big-timers. He gave me as much time as I wanted and answered every question as though his answers were actually going to be heard by more than a few hundred people.

I can't explain how much that meant to me.

The one thing that scared me the most when I was starting out was interviewing big-name athletes. In June of 1973 there was nobody on the planet bigger than Jack Nicklaus and he couldn't have been nicer. I left there that day thinking, "They don't get any bigger than this guy. If I can interview Jack Nicklaus, I can interview anybody."

When we got back to the station I told the station owner that we got a one-on-one with Jack Nicklaus and she was thrilled.

We put the tape in the machine to play it back and the picture was upside down.

It never made the air.

WHILE WE'RE ON THE SUBJECT

I got my first of many up-close-and-personal moments with Arnold Palmer at that 1971 Firestone Classic in Akron. Actually, it wasn't all that personal. I guess it was the first close-up look. I remember being shocked by how athletic Palmer looked. He would have been 41 years old at the time and he was built like a linebacker with huge shoulders and forearms. I also watched him wade through the crowd after he came off 18 and sign hundreds of autographs. He could have easily avoided the crowd by taking a different route but he didn't.

(I'm thinking that Tiger Woods almost always takes the different route.)

Palmer wasn't a factor in the tournament but he made the biggest impression on me when he left. Or, I should say, with how he left.

Firestone Country Club is only about five minutes away from the Akron-Canton Airport and Akron is close enough to Latrobe that Arnie was commuting back and forth. A short time after he disappeared from the parking lot, a big crowd was gathered near the 18th green. I can't remember why, but it could have been because the leader, Jerry Heard was finishing his round.

All of a sudden there is a loud roar and out of nowhere comes a low-flying jet. It seemed like it was at tree top level.

It was Arnie.

He flew right over the top of the 18th green, did a quick bank and a climb and then tipped his wings.

Very cool.

The crowd went nuts.

It's still the most impressive exit I've ever seen an athlete make.

Little did I know that 11 years later I would be flying with Palmer in his jet on the way to another golf tournament in Ohio.

WHILE WE'RE STILL ON THE SUBJECT

My first (and only) up-close-and-personal moment with Tiger Woods was much different. It was at the grand opening of the Mystic Rock course at Joe Hardy's Nemacolin Resort in 1996. Woods was in his first year on the tour and was there to play an exhibition round. He was paired with Pennsylvania Governor Tom Ridge. I was standing in a large crowd about two feet away from Woods and Ridge as they waited to tee off on the first hole. Ridge tapped Woods on the shoulder and held out a golf ball and said, "Tiger, would you mind signing this for my son?"

Woods, who was 20 or 21 at the time, looked over his shoulder at Ridge and said, "I don't sign golf balls." This was the governor of Pennsylvania, in front of several people, asking him to sign a golf ball and Tiger blew him off. Ridge was obviously embarrassed and I'm sure at least a little pissed off.

Sorry, but I think of that every time I see Tiger on TV and I find it really hard to root for him.

Apparently, Tiger doesn't stick to his game plan as strictly when it comes to his marriage vows. In December of 2009, he had a little problem with women claiming that they had joined him for some twosomes that had nothing to do with golf.

Have you ever seen Tiger's wife?

If par is 72, she's a 58.

Bad move, Tiger.

It should be pretty obvious to anyone who has watched Woods on the golf course that he's a self-absorbed guy. He's amazingly good at turning his focus inward and that has been a factor in his success on the course. It's also another reason why I've had a tough time rooting for him. He doesn't look like he's having much fun out there. I realize that it's a game that requires intense concentration, but it's also a game that has a lot of dead time between the "action." Jack Nicklaus, Gary Player, Tom Watson, Greg Norman and Arnold Palmer all seemed to be able to mix in a smile every now and then, and not only when things were going well.

Nicklaus played for over 40 years and I don't ever remember seeing him slam a club on the ground or drop a lip-reader's F-bomb. Tiger does both on a regular basis. I've always felt Tiger was wound a little too tightly and needed someone to come up to him while he was walking down the fairway, tap him on the shoulder and say, "Tiger, it's only golf."

CHAPTER 5

POSING FOR PLAYBOY

I haven't believed anything that I've read in Playboy Magazine since 1972. Not since I appeared in that year's College Preview issue. That's not to say that I haven't glanced at an issue or two from time to time since then.

It started with three ice cubes on Chris Johnson's bare chest.

Chris was a Kent State student from Scott Township and he was lying shirtless on the floor of his campus high-rise apartment. His roommate, Tom, also from Scott Township, decided to empty the ice from his drink on to Johnson's chest.

Johnson refused to give his roommate the satisfaction of letting him know that the ice bothered him and he said, "You can have everybody dump ice on my chest. It won't bother me."

It escalated from there.

Within about half an hour, Johnson was sitting in the bathtub and ice was being brought in from other apartments to pour over top of him.

Somebody mentioned the Guinness Book of World Records and then it really got crazy.

Don't ask me how, but the Guinness people were contacted and Chris and Tom and the rest of the mob that had gathered to watch the spectacle found out that there either was no record for time spent covered with ice or the record that did exist was definitely breakable.

I was working at WKSU-FM, the Kent State radio station, and got wind of what was going on and, since we subscribed to the Associated Press wire service, I decided to give the AP a call to see if they were interested in the story.

They were and pretty soon the story of Chris Johnson trying to set or break a world record was being sent around the world.

I got a call from Pittsburgh and was told that Bill Burns had reported the story on KDKA and had even added one of his snide remarks. It was reported in the Pittsburgh Press and the Post-Gazette and hundreds of newspapers around the country.

I don't remember how long Chris stayed buried in ice but he was given credit for doing it longer than anyone else in human history.

A few months later Playboy magazine came calling.

Hef and the gang were putting together the 1972 back-to-college issue and they were doing a story on the most recent college fads.

Remember, this was Kent State, a school that had gone from being obscure to world-famous less than two years earlier when four students were shot and killed by the National Guard. If not for the notoriety from that, Playboy almost certainly would not have paid any attention to Johnson's story.

Without interviewing anybody involved, Playboy had decided that students burying themselves in ice was the latest fad on the Kent State campus. Of course, nothing could have been further from the truth.

Chris Johnson was the only one who had done it and there were rumors going around that he may have cheated and not stayed under ice as long as the people at Guinness were led to believe.

Playboy was obviously not interested in letting the truth get in the way of a good story. A photo shoot was set for March near an area on campus called The Commons, where the shootings had taken place. Since I was responsible for the story getting worldwide coverage, I was included in the photo shoot, along with a few other guys and my friend Goose, who was not there for Johnson's world-record performance and was not a Kent State student, but refused to miss out on a chance to be in Playboy.

We were told that a topless woman would be getting into a bathtub full of ice and that we were supposed to be standing by looking at our watches as though we were timing her. I don't remember anybody being late for the shoot.

It was spitting snow when the bathtub and several pounds of ice were placed outside near The Commons and we all stood around waiting for the arrival of the model, who had been hired by Playboy through an Akron modeling agency.

Keep in mind that this is a story about Kent State students who were caught up in a whacky fad that had spread across campus.

The model arrived in a limo.

She was paid $25.

Cardboard boxes were placed in the tub before she got in so that she would be protected from the ice.

She sat down, took off her shirt to reveal breasts that were slightly bigger than mine and several pictures were taken.

Find a copy of the September, 1972, issue of Playboy and you'll see the picture right there on page 102. The caption says that the latest craze sweeping the Kent State campus is students burying themselves in ice.

In the picture, you can see that Goose and I are looking at our watches, but we also have our thumbs pointing outward in the "get outta here" position because we couldn't believe what a fraud the whole thing was.

In the magazine, there are also stories of all the crazy things being done at other colleges around the country, including a story about kids sunbathing on rooftops in the nude. I, of course, knew that all the "roofers" in the story were models who had been paid $25.

That was 38 years ago and I haven't believed a word that I've read in Playboy since.

Chris Johnson, who may or may not still hold that record, drowned in Lake Erie several years later.

WHILE WE'RE ON THE SUBJECT

The two guys who were involved in the Ice Capade, Chris and Tom, were also involved in one of the best practical joke/prank battles in American college history.

It all started innocently enough with some guys across town having a pizza delivered to Tom and Chris, which was followed by a much larger order of pizzas being ordered across town. Let's call the guys across town Walt and Steve, since I'm not 100 percent sure exactly who was living in that house at the time. Everybody involved was from Pittsburgh, I can tell you that.

The pizza war went on for a while and eventually included hoagies, salad and who knows what else.

Then Walt and Steve got an idea.

At the time, part-time jobs were extremely hard to come by at Kent State. Any business that did have an opening would be immediately swamped with applicants.

Walt and Steve put an ad in the "Kent Stater," the campus newspaper that was read by just about everybody.

It looked like this:

JOBS! JOBS! JOBS!
CALL 216-555-1234

It was the phone number for Chris and Tom's apartment.

Their phone didn't stop ringing for days.

Then things got interesting.

Instead of telling the callers that they had been used in a practical joke, Chris and Tom started telling the callers that there were jobs to be had and they set up interviews at Walt and Steve's house.

Pretty soon, kids wearing coats and ties started showing up at Walt and Steve's for their job interview.

I don't remember how it ended but I do remember one of the guys telling me that, no matter what they said the job was, the callers would try to convince them that they were qualified.

Including one kid who said he was the perfect guy for the chicken coop-cleaning position since his grandmother had always raised chickens.

I don't know how he did in his interview.

CHAPTER 6

LOOK OUT, CURT GOWDY

IN June of 1972 my pathetic college career had come to an end. I had attended four colleges in six years and had no degree and it was time to get a job. Despite my abuse of the concept of a college education, I felt a lot more fortunate than the guys I knew who actually graduated in 1972. I can remember asking them a few months earlier what they planned to do when they graduated and almost all of them had no idea. Most of them would be going to employment agencies and throwing themselves at the mercy of Corporate America.

I was going after Curt Gowdy's job.

Gowdy was the Big Guy at NBC sports. He called the World Series and the Super Bowl and he was the No. 1 announcer for regular season Major League Baseball and NFL games. The word was he was making $300,000 a year.

That's the job I wanted.

I've always been a pretty creative guy and I came up with a brilliant plan about six months earlier while I was at Kent State.

I dropped out.

I know. That's been done before. The difference was, I didn't tell anybody at the school. I had figured out that, when I went to NBC looking for Curt Gowdy's job, there was a pretty good chance they weren't going to ask me what I got in biology.

Or geology.

Or economics.

They were going to ask to see and/or hear a tape. Here I am, almost 40 years later, and still nobody has asked me about those nine biology credits that I needed for my degree in telecommunications. I decided to hang around Kent's campus and pretend that I was a student. That gave me access to the campus radio and TV stations. I realized that it might not be fair to the kids who were paying tuition but I justified it by taking into account all the money that good ol' KSU had taken from me for courses that had nothing to do with what I planned to do with my life.

I remembered the TV Production class that I took, taught by Dr. Thozewhookant, in which we spent weeks — and I mean weeks — learning how to draw a cornucopia in case we ever got a job in a TV station art department and needed to make a really nice color slide for a station ID. Back then, an artist would actually draw pictures that were turned into slides that were used as background for messages from the station.

I wondered why a class of 30 or 40, made up of people with all kinds of ideas about what areas of broadcasting they wanted to pursue, would be forced to waste their time and money on something that ridiculous. Apparently, I was one of very few who wondered. That's how colleges get away with making parents spend huge amounts of money so their kids can waste huge amounts of time.

Since I no longer had to go to class, I had all the time in the world to devote to working at the campus facilities. I did a jazz show on WKSU, the FM station that had a 50-mile radius and actually had real live human beings listening to it. I did sportscasts on the closed-circuit AM station that could only be heard in the dormitories and was only listened to by some of the people who were within a 50-foot radius of the studio. I did play-by-play of Kent State baseball games on WKSU-FM (I remember describing a home run by a guy named Ken Macha, who played for Pitt). I also did play-by-play of Kent State basketball and color for Kent State hockey on the campus closed-circuit TV station.

Good old WKSU proved to be a pretty good proving ground. Larry Clisby, who split the basketball duties with me, has been the radio voice of Purdue basketball for close to 30 years. Mike Fornes and Steve Albert were the two hockey play-by-play announcers. Fornes went on to spend several years calling Washington Capitals games. Albert, whose brothers Marv and Al have done OK for themselves, graduated from Kent State and immediately took a job doing the World Hockey Association Cleveland Crusaders on 50,000-watt 3WE. Steve Albert shared the WKSU baseball booth with me (it was an abandoned bus that sat in foul territory down the right field line). He also spent several years doing TV play-by-play for the New York Mets.

I never once saw him in women's clothes or heard him singing Broadway show tunes, by the way....

Before I left Kent State, I used the radio studio there to produce a tape that I hoped to use to get my first job. I actually used a portion of the play-by-play printout of the Kent State-Iowa State football game from the previous season to re-create a game. That Iowa State team was coached by some guy named Johnny Majors.

So I was ready for that first job. All I had to do was get somebody to listen to the tape. I knew that they would be so impressed that I would have to sort through the offers.

I sent out cover letters to 200 stations around the country and enclosed a self-addressed post card that gave the recipient the option of checking a box that said:

- INTERESTED
- NOT INTERESTED
- INTERESTED, NO OPENING NOW, PLEASE SEND TAPE AND RESUME
- INTERESTED, IMMEDIATE OPENING, PLEASE SEND TAPE AND RESUME

I got about 50 responses and all but one was marked NOT INTERESTED. The station that was interested was in Roswell, New Mexico, and they were looking for someone to read farm reports at five in the morning. (And maybe keep an eye out for UFOs.)

Keep in mind that Roswell was one of the biggest markets on my list.

In the meantime, I took a job selling cable TV door-to-door in Bethel Park. Hey, it was TV, right? I couldn't believe how much money I was making. We were required to keep track of the hours we worked and I never went over 18 in a week and I never made less than $250. That's about $1,300 in 2010 dollars. I went out and bought a brand new, baby-blue Triumph Spitfire. I paid $2,950 for it and my payments were $90 per month.

Back before I left Kent State, I had heard rumors about a new TV station starting up in Pittsburgh in my neighborhood. Mt. Lebanon Cable TV was just getting started and part of the plan was a TV station that would produce local news, sports and entertainment programs.

I was all over it. I bugged the general manager every day. He told me that I was exactly the kind of guy he was looking for. I would work for next to nothing and I grew up in the area. After three months of waiting, the station went on the air.

I didn't get the job.

The number one job went to a kid (let's call him Walt) who knew Sam Nover, who, at the time, was a big-time sportscaster on Channel 11. Nover knew the Mt. Lebanon general manager and put in the good word for Walt. I knew Walt wasn't as good as I was but I sucked it up and signed on to be his sidekick.

For nothing.

It was a good lesson in the ways of broadcasting. Fortunately, I was still pulling in the cash going door-to-door selling cable and driving around in a really nice sports car.

We thought we would be doing play-by-play of Mt. Lebanon High School's sports but the school district was worried about the effect on attendance at their games and wouldn't give us permission.

Keep in mind that the games were going to be taped — not live — and, at the time, Mt. Lebanon Cable TV had about 300 subscribers.

That was a good lesson in government stupidity.

So Walt and I did the Keystone Oaks High School basketball games.

That was a good lesson in broadcasting stupidity.

Keystone Oaks is next to Mt. Lebanon but there were no Mt. Lebanon Cable subscribers in any of the neighborhoods that fed the KO school district. So, how many of those 300 subscribers do you suppose tuned in to those KO games? I probably had more viewers on the Kent State closed-circuit TV station.

Even back then, I couldn't believe the stupidity of the decision. It seemed to me that not doing any games at all would be better than doing the games of a rival school. It was the first time that I was involved in a TV station making a decision that took everybody but the viewers into account. It wouldn't be the last.

Curt Gowdy's job was safe.

Meanwhile, my former college broadcaster buddies were getting jobs. Albert got the Cleveland Crusaders job and Larry Clisby, using the same post card method that I had used, landed a job in Paducah, Kentucky, doing high school football and basketball and also calling the games for Paducah Junior College. I would have killed for that job.

We used to hear all the time at WKSU that, in order to make it in this business, you have to be willing to go anywhere, even if it means Paducah, to get a job. My buddy Clisby actually took a job in Paducah.

I heard about another kid from WKSU landing a job in Rome, Georgia, doing Little League baseball and high school sports. Another job I would have killed for.

Not long into my tenure as Walt's sidekick at Mt. Lebanon Cable TV, Walt dropped a "yinz" on the air. I don't remember the context, but does it matter? After two or three more "yinzes" I knew I had to go out and find a real job. Well, not a real, real job. A real broadcasting job.

Of course, years later Sam Nover and I became good friends and I never once heard him say "yinz." On the air or off.

So what's the moral of this story? Often it's not what you know but who you know and a college degree is one of the most overrated things on the planet.

CHAPTER 7

SHORT STOP
FREE INSTALLATION

I may be one of the greatest cable-TV door-to-door salesmen in history. I was also one of the fastest grocery bag packers of all time. Those were two jobs that I depended on more than once on my way to broadcast greatness. Selling cable was quite an adventure. I went into neighborhoods I otherwise would never have seen in places like Monessen and McKeesport, not to mention Hamilton, Ohio.

If you live in Monessen, Bethel Park, McKeesport, Charleroi, Green Tree or Scott Township, there's a decent chance that I introduced you to the wonders of cable-TV. It wasn't always an easy sell. My first go-around was in 1972 in Bethel Park. I was paid $10 for every yes that I got to my offer of a free installation. I never worked more than 18 hours and never made less than $250 a week, the equivalent of over $1,200 per week in 2010 dollars. It's hard to imagine life without cable-TV now, but almost nobody had it back then. My sales pitch began with pointing to the silver cables across the street and explaining to the potential customer that the cable company would be running a wire from there to the back of the customer's TV and that it would result in perfect TV reception.

I did well but it was amazing how many people just refused to accept the idea of paying for TV. I promised them WOR-TV from New York and Channel 43 from Cleveland, which meant New York Mets games and lots of old movies. A few people refused to consider it because they were sure it was a way for the government to spy on them through their televisions.

When I couldn't find another baseball job after the 1976 season with the Charleston Charlies, I decided to give selling cable another shot. This time I started in McKeesport. The sales manager, Paul Rotstein, gave me a speech about what I should say when someone answered the door and told me to make sure I wore a tie.

I ignored him on both counts and became, by far, his best salesman. I didn't want to look like a salesman and I thought I could do much better by just talking to people instead of giving them a canned speech. It was the same philosophy I used in my broadcasting career. I did whatever I could to not sound like a sportscaster.

A few years into my TV career I even tried the no-tie approach on camera and wore sweaters.

I made $20,000 selling cable TV from September 1976 until August of 1977. That would be over $70,000 in 2010 dollars.

Not bad for a door-to-door salesman. I wonder if the Fuller Brush Man ever made that much. I've always found it interesting that before I started coming into people's living rooms by way of their television, I came into the living rooms of thousands of people to talk to them about their television.

I always wondered how many people, when they saw my mug show up on WTAE a year and a half later said, "Hey, there's that guy who sold (or tried to sell) us the cable."

I got so good at selling the product that when someone would turn me down I would tell them to remember that I was there offering free installation because some day they would have cable-TV and have to pay a lot more to have it installed.

They would say, "No I won't, I'll never pay for TV." I would smile and say, "Oh, yes you will."

Who do you think won that argument?

I was out knocking on doors in Monessen during the Winter of 1977, one of the worst Western Pennsylvania winters on record. The one no-sale that sticks out in my mind happened in one of Monessen's best neighborhoods. It was a nice Tudor with one of those four-feet thick, wooden front doors.

The temperature was probably in the teens, the wind was blowing and it was snowing. I rang the doorbell and waited for someone to open the inside door. After a couple of minutes I heard an old woman say from behind the door, "Yes. Can I help you?"

I said, "I'm from the cable-TV office, can I talk to you for a minute?"

"What?" she said.

The blowing snow was hitting my face.

"I'm from the cable-TV office, we're offering free installation. Can I talk to you for a minute?"

"What?" she said through the four feet thick door.

My eyelids were starting to freeze shut.

"I want to talk to you about cable-TV."

"What?"

"I want to talk to you about cable-TV."

By now I was a minute or two from dying of hypothermia and the nice old lady said this: "I have a table for my TV."

To which I replied, "OK, ma'am, just checking."

Even in 1977, not everybody was familiar or comfortable with the concept of cable-TV.

My brother Paul got the best response I've ever heard from an uninterested customer. He had heard that I was making a pretty good buck and decided to give selling cable a try while he was looking for a real job.

I think the response came from a guy in Carnegie. Paul gave him the spiel about how he would get much better reception on the local stations and when that wasn't enough to close the deal, he told the guy that he would also be getting WOR out of New York.

The guy said, "I don't know nobody in New York."

How are you going to argue with that? Paul thanked him and walked away.

I saw a lot of interesting sights inside people's homes.

A nice couple living on the main drag in Charleroi invited me in to show me the orangutan they kept in a cage in the living room. They also had a chimpanzee in a cage in the dining room.

They went for the free installation. I made the sale.

And back then there was no Animal Planet.

I was always amused by the people who said, "We never watch TV."

I don't think I ever heard that line come from someone whose TV was not on at the time. They would say that to me and I would just raise an eyebrow and nod toward the TV.

All in all, being a door-to-door salesman was a great experience and it reinforced in me something that I have always believed and something that contributed to my success in TV and radio: When someone lets you into their home, the best way to get them to trust you is to keep it real.

CHAPTER 8

TWO BUCKS AN HOUR

SOMETIMES it's just about being in the right place at the right time. In the winter of 1972 I had been selling cable TV door-to-door and making a ridiculous amount of money for very little work, but I was pretty sure I didn't want to be still knocking on doors in 2002. I was still sending out letters to small radio stations all over the United States and getting no response. My friend, Joe Butler, who founded and still operates the Metro Index Scouting Service, asked me to go with him to a coaches clinic at the William Penn Hotel.

It was a big deal, attended by some of the biggest names in college football, including Bear Bryant.

I didn't have a lot going on so I decided to check it out. I ran into a guy named Lee Cicco, who had been a year ahead of me at South Hills Catholic High School and he asked me what I was doing. When I told him that I was trying to get my first broadcasting job on my way to taking Curt Gowdy's away from him, he told me about a cable TV station in Sharon, Pa., where he was coaching high school football. It was called Color Channel 3 and was owned by a 59-year-old woman named Loraine Yuhasz. Cicco said that they video taped and replayed all the high school games up there in the Shenango Valley and they were doing a 6 and 11 o'clock newscast six nights a week.

This was a local station that was way ahead of its time.

I decided to check it out. When Mrs. Yuhasz asked me what I wanted to do, I told her I wanted Curt Gowdy's job, but working for Color

Channel 3 would do for now. She said something about being happy as a big fish in a small pond, but I didn't want to hear it.

She hired me.

For $2 an hour.

I had bought a new sports car less than two months earlier and I was making $250 for working 18 hours a week selling cable. This was something I had to think about. I thought for about four seconds and said, "Deal."

When I got back to Pittsburgh, my dad asked me how it went and I said that it went well. He asked me how much the job paid and when I told him $2 an hour, he laughed and said, "You told her to forget it, right?"

I said, "Nope, I start Tuesday."

He told me I was nuts but I knew it was the perfect job for me.

I don't know what it's like in 2010, but when I started out in broadcasting you had to be willing to do anything anywhere for any amount of money in order to get that first job. I didn't care about the money. I knew I was going to be doing the play-by-play of three high school football games every weekend and several high school basketball games a week and I would be sitting in front of a camera doing a sportscast twice a day, six times a week.

When I talk to kids who are starting out now, I tell them that they should separate themselves from the pack by having the willingness to go anywhere for just about any price.

A lot of kids won't be willing to do that and, in a field as competitive as sports broadcasting, you're picky at your own peril. Let the other guy be the one to give up because he doesn't want to move far away from home. That's one less guy you have to beat out on your way to the big time.

I tell them to look at the $21,000 a year job in Keokuk, Iowa, as their graduate school. It's one more year of learning, but instead of paying someone another $21,000 to teach you, someone pays you to learn. You're $42,000 to the good. Plus, you get a start on your resume and more important your demo tape.

The first month on the job at Color Channel 3, I commuted back and forth from Kent, Ohio, because my brother, Paul, who was a student at Kent State at the time, had told me about an empty dorm room on his floor. I was able to sleep and shower there for free.

I eventually moved into a trailer — not a mobile home, a trailer — that was parked in someone's backyard way out in the country between Sharon and Mercer, Pa. It was a steal for 75 bucks a month.

The Color Channel 3 studios were in an old, Civil War-era mansion in Clark, Pa., several miles north of Sharon. At this writing it's being used as a restaurant called Tara. We did play-by-play of football, boys and girls basketball and wrestling for Sharon, Farrell, Hickory, Greenville, Reynolds, Sharpsville and West Middlesex high schools and probably a few more that I don't remember.

Before the football games I would help with the building of our scaffolding and I'd help tear it down after the game. All for two bucks an hour.

I learned a lot about how people in those areas felt about high school sports. It was much different from what I was used to. Growing up in the South Hills of Pittsburgh, most guys cared about their high school teams a lot while they were in high school and for two or three years after they graduated.

Up there in the northwest I noticed 35-year-old guys wearing their high school letter jackets. That's not a criticism. That's the way it is in most of America and it took me a long time to realize it, but towns like Sharon, Pa., are America and they're what's great about America.

To the people in the Shenango Valley, the Sharon-Farrell basketball game was Duke-North Carolina. There were bookies in nearby Youngstown who were happy to take bets on the game. Farrell had Eddie McCluskey, who the previous year had won his seventh state championship, still a Pennsylvania record. He had been coaching Farrell since 1949 and would continue until 1977 and still holds the record with 11 WPIAL titles, despite playing in conferences that included schools two or three times the size of Farrell. He was as revered in The Valley as Chuck Noll is revered in Pittsburgh.

I eventually learned that the farther you get outside the city, the more intense the rivalries and the more interesting the games become.

Sharon-Farrell basketball games were always sold out and there was always a lot of ticket scalping going on. So I thought it was pretty cool to be calling the play-by-play even though the game was going to be shown on tape delay later that night. I knew it would get a huge audience in The Valley.

High school football was big there, too, but basketball was king. Sharon's star player was a kid named Randy Holloway, who also played football and became an All-America defensive end at Pitt and had a long and successful career with the Minnesota Vikings.

Things slowed down quite a bit in The Valley in the summer. We did a few Little League playoff games and that was about it. I still had my 6 and 11 o'clock sportscasts to do and I included the Pirates in my sportscasts. In April of 1973 I got my first press pass for a Pirates game. It was opening day and it was also the day that Roberto Clemente's number was officially retired. He had died a little over three months before and there was a moving ceremony at home plate when his wife, Vera, and his three sons were presented with his jersey.

I couldn't believe I was allowed to be there on the field, only a few feet away. Little did I know that, several years later, Vera would take me on a tour of their home in Puerto Rico and show me all of Clemente's mementos and awards that were literally piled up in her basement.

I started thinking about my next job five minutes after I started my first one and I had decided to do sports commentaries as part of my sportscasts because I wanted to have evidence of my brilliant writing style.

In the summer of 1973, the Pirates fired their manager, Bill Virdon, and replaced him with Danny Murtaugh, even though Virdon had come within a wild pitch of going to the World Series in 1972.

I figured it was time for me to do a hard-hitting commentary and I ripped the Pirates. I thought I had done a great job of proving that they had screwed Virdon and I was sure that anybody who was watching had to have been impressed. I was feeling pretty good about myself and wondering why the Pittsburgh stations hadn't heard about me and offered me a job.

About five minutes after I had done my devastating commentary that I was sure was already reverberating its way down I-79 to Pittsburgh, my boss, Lorraine, visited me at my desk. I could tell that she was excited and I was sure that she had seen the commentary and wanted to tell me how great it was. Or I thought maybe she was there to tell me that KDKA had called and asked about my contract status.

I was wrong.

Some kid had caught a really big fish in the reservoir next to the station and she wanted me to do an interview with him.

Talk about crashing to Earth.

I did the interview and made a big deal about it and decided then and there that I had to move on. A big fish had convinced me that I still had no interest in being a big fish in a little pond.

WHILE WE'RE ON THE SUBJECT

I can't do a chapter on Sharon without talking about the biggest catch of my life. A few months after I started working for Color Channel 3, I met the woman who would become my wife a year later. And, believe it or not, Jeani is still with me after more than 36 years. I guess that gets us back to it being all about being in the right place at the right time.

CHAPTER 9

THANKS A LOT, JACK

I was never interested in being a big fish in the Shenango Valley pond and I considered everything I did there at Color Channel 3 in Sharon, Pa., to be nothing more than preparation for my next job. In 1974 I had gotten a raise from my starting salary of $2 an hour to $460 a month, so I wasn't too worried about finding a job that would involve another pay cut.

I was still interested in Curt Gowdy's job and I thought the quickest route would be by becoming the play-by-play man for a Major League Baseball team.

I knew I would first have to prove myself in the minor leagues.

Unfortunately, almost all of my play-by-play experience the past several months had been in football and basketball. I had done a few Little League games but I didn't think I would impress anybody with the tapes of those games since they consisted of one camera shot and my announcer's booth was on top of the cab of a pickup truck that had been donated by the station owner's brother in law.

One thing you learn on your way to Curt Gowdy's job is that his job is a lot easier than yours. Most people don't stop to consider that it's a lot easier to call Game 7 of the World Series from behind home plate at Yankee Stadium than it is to call a quarterfinal game in the West Middlesex Youth Baseball tournament from the top of a pickup truck.

(I think it was West Middlesex, but don't hold me to it.)

Curt had six or eight cameras, producers giving him information in his ear and graphics with more statistics than he would ever need. And Tony Kubek.

I had 60-year-old amateur photographer Ted Rogalny precariously perched on top of a pickup truck with a black-and-white video camera, sitting on a flimsy tripod and a plastic, hand-held microphone.

I didn't have a lot of stats to work with and I had no color analyst.

To get a baseball play-by-play job you need a tape of yourself calling a game and I wasn't about to subject a minor league general manager to my greatest hits from the West Middlesex Youth Baseball Championship, so I had to go to my master plan.

I called the Pirates.

I had found Pirates Media Relations Director Bill Guilfoyle to be an amazingly nice guy when I had bothered him for press credentials. He took my position with Color Channel 3 seriously. At least he did a great job of acting like he did. I told him that I desperately needed to make a baseball tape and I asked him if I could use an empty radio booth at Three Rivers Stadium to record a Pirates game.

Amazingly enough, he said yes. I have a feeling that that wouldn't happen today.

I showed up at Three Rivers Stadium with my tape recorder and I took the Pirates' press handout and stats and headed for my booth to call the Pirates and the Phillies.

Steve Carlton threw a two-hitter and the Pirates lost, 2-1.

Two hitters by Steve Carlton are nice but they don't afford aspiring play-by-play guys a lot of opportunities to show what they can do. Most people probably think that baseball is the easiest sport to do because there's not much continuous action.

Wrong.

Baseball, by far, is the most difficult because of all the dead spots.

I managed to get two pretty good innings out of it. Now, all I had to do was figure out who to send it to and how to get it there.

Bill Guilfoyle came through again. He suggested I call Bill Turner, an old guy who had been working in the Pirates minor league system for years. Bill couldn't have been nicer and he invited me to his office to use his "Blue Book."

There was no Internet and no Google in 1973, so if you wanted to find information on minor league baseball teams, you had to go to the "Blue Book," which could only be found in the offices of professional baseball teams. I spent hours in Turner's office at Three Rivers Stadium writing down phone numbers and the names of the general managers of as many teams from "A" ball to "AAA" as I could and headed back to Sharon.

Let's just say that the response I got on the other end of my phone calls was not all that enthusiastic. Most of the general managers were nice but they all said I needed more experience.

During a call to John Wallenstein, the general manager of the Wichita Aeros, I mentioned that I was frustrated by my lack of experience doing baseball. I told him that there are very few places in the country where a guy can get experience doing high school or college baseball. I told him that I had plenty of football and basketball experience and asked how I could get the baseball experience I needed if nobody in the minor leagues would give me a shot.

Then Wallenstein made a big mistake.

He told me that maybe I should just be obnoxious and keep hounding the general managers until I found one who would give me a shot.

Boy, did I hound the shit out of John Wallenstein.

I told him I would pay my own way to Wichita and I would do Aeros games for nothing and work in a gas station during the day if that's what he wanted.

Then Wallenstein made another mistake.

He invited me to come out to Wichita — on my dime, of course.

I was met at the airport by Wallenstein, his assistant GM Bob Drew and a very strange looking old man with Joe Paterno glasses named Joe Ryan, who was president of the American Association.

The Wichita Aeros were a Triple A team, an affiliate of the Chicago Cubs. I would have actually preferred a chance to meet with a Class "A" team because I thought I had a better chance of getting the job but I was thrilled to be in Wichita.

The position had opened up because the guy who had been calling their games on radio, Larry Calton, had been hired to do the Minnesota Twins games.

I wanted this job.

I was told by Assistant GM Drew that he and Wallenstein liked my tape, my enthusiasm and my look. I had over-the-ear length hair and a Fu Man Chu moustache. Apparently, they were going after the youth market. I was also told that I was one of two finalists for the job.

While I was sitting in the office with Drew, the phone rang. Drew answered it and said, "Oh, Hi Jack. Yeah, thanks for calling. We really appreciate it. I promise we'll give him strong consideration. He's one of the two finalists."

I didn't know who Jack was but I knew he wasn't calling to recommend me.

Bob Drew hangs up the phone and says, "That was Jack Buck. He called to recommend the other finalist."

Yeah, *that* Jack Buck.

I figured I was done.

I went back to Sharon thinking that I would be doing one more season on top of the pickup truck, but a few days later I got a call from Bob Drew. He asked me if I was still interested in the job.

Dumb question.

He asked if $600 a month would be enough. I told him I would have paid him $600 a month to let me call the games.

The job was mine. I was in shock.

A few weeks later I was in Wichita getting ready to go to the Cubs' spring training complex in Scottsdale, Arizona, and I got around to asking Drew why I got the job over the guy who was recommended by Jack Buck. Drew said, "John (Wallenstein) really liked your persistence and your enthusiasm. He also liked your interview with Chuck Tanner."

Earlier that winter, Tanner, who was from nearby New Castle, made an appearance in Sharon and I got him to do a sit-down interview. At the time, Tanner was considered the hottest, young manager in baseball. He had done wonders with the Chicago White Sox. I don't remember the interview being anything special, but it was special to the guy who made the decision that changed my life forever,

It turned out that John Wallenstein was from Chicago and a *huge* White Sox fan.

Of course, a few years later I was dealing with Tanner on a regular basis at Three Rivers Stadium and he became one of my all-time favorites.

If Wallenstein is a Cubs fan, I don't get the job.

Oh, by the way, you might have heard of the other finalist for that Aeros play-by-play job. His name is Jon Miller.

You may have heard him do a game or two on ESPN.

WHILE WE'RE ON THE SUBJECT

In 2000 I finally got a chance to talk to Jon Miller about beating him out for the Wichita Aero job. He was in Pittsburgh to do a game for ESPN and I ran into him in the press lounge. I introduced myself and said, "Do you remember applying for a job with the Wichita Aeros back in 1974?" He said he did and I laughed and told him that I was the guy who beat him out. Miller had long established himself as one of the best play-by-play guys in baseball with the Orioles and Giants and here he was on the verge of becoming a big star with ESPN. I figured he would find it interesting to finally run into the guy who beat him out for his first job. I might have said something to the effect of, "Whatever happened to you after that. Did you ever find work?" I thought he might get a little chuckle out of it.

What a jagoff.

Miller grunted and made his way to the food line.

It's really amazing how many miserable people there are in this world.

I couldn't think of a job I'd want less than his, by the way. My career was much more interesting because I saw so much more than baseball. I also never liked listening to him. Like 99 percent of the baseball announcers on the planet, he's pompous and boring.

Jack Buck notwithstanding.

CHAPTER 10

LIFE ON THE FARM

I N my 37 years of being paid to watch sports, there was nothing I enjoyed more than my three years doing minor league baseball play-by-play.

Wichita 1974

My soon-to-be-wife Jeani and I drove to Wichita in the old Triumph Spitfire that I bought for $500 after I realized that I couldn't afford the new one with my $2 an hour salary. It wouldn't start unless I sprayed ether into the carburetor and the passenger-side window wouldn't close all the way and that made things a little uncomfortable when we were going 65 miles per hour on the interstate. It was late February, 1974.

I learned a lot about a lot of things in my three years of riding the buses in the minors. I lived in three very different areas of the country and learned a lot about the world outside of Western Pennsylvania.

For example, I learned that there is only one tree in Kansas that is visible from the interstate. That is some flat, desolate country out there. I also learned that people in Kansas really, really like to eat meat. Cow meat. Man, were there a lot of steakhouses. It didn't take long to figure out that it gets hot in the middle of Kansas. It was the first place I had ever been where ramshackle houses and dilapidated cars had air-conditioning. I noticed that before it got hot. In 1974, an air-conditioned car was a luxury in Western Pa. and very few people had air-conditioned homes. It didn't take long for me to find out why all the old shacks had air conditioners in several windows.

I can remember sitting in the radio booth behind home plate at Lawrence Stadium and watching the temperature flashing at the top of Wichita's tallest building.

98... 98... 98...

And that was after dark. The sidewalks outside Lawrence Stadium were still warm after night games.

I had no idea what to expect when it came to the games themselves. The only professional baseball games I had ever seen were major league games played in major league ballparks and two of those were in Pittsburgh, the other in Cleveland.

It was love at first sight.

The Aeros had always drawn well in Wichita and the stadium was packed on opening night. I realized right away that a 10,000-seat ballpark with 10,000 people and two Triple "A" teams in it made for a much better baseball experience than a 50,000-seat football stadium with 15,000 people and two major league teams in it.

I also realized right away that I was going to be seeing some really good baseball. On most nights, if you put major league uniforms on two Triple "A" teams, except for the fact that you missed the star players, you would think you were watching a major league game.

As the season went along, I also learned a lot about the politics of baseball and I'm sure it was the same then as it was in 1924 and it's the same now.

The Aeros were the Triple "A" affiliate of the Cubs, who had a well-earned reputation for employing scouts and coaches for all the wrong reasons. Most of them were former Cubs who had ingratiated themselves to the right people in the Cubs' front office.

The Aeros had a kid playing first base named Ron Matney. He was a good-fielding switch hitter whose batting average from both sides of the plate stayed right around .330 all year after he had hit .325 in Wichita the year before.

When I would talk to Cubs coaches and scouts they would tell me, off the record, of course, that he wasn't a prospect. When the season ended the first week of September, Matney wasn't called up to the Cubs but a .230 hitter named Gene Hiser was.

Hiser was a left hand-hitting centerfielder whose batting average stayed around .230 all year.

Every scout and coach told me Hiser was a prospect.

So, how can a guy who hits .330 be sent home in September and a guy who hits .230 get a call up to the Cubs?

Easy answer.

Hiser was a Number One draft pick.

Somewhere in the Cubs organization there was a scout whose reputation was on the line for having recommended picking Hiser in the first round. Matney was either a low-round pick or signed as a free agent. Calling him up to the big leagues would have marked him as a prospect and the scouts couldn't have that because they had been calling him a non-prospect for years.

Matney never got a chance in the big leagues.

Hiser, who had hit .174 in 71 games for the Cubs in 1973, finished his career in 1975 with a lifetime batting average of .202 in 206 games. He got chance after chance to prove the scouts right, but the same scouts had no interest in letting Ron Matney prove them wrong. I can guarantee you that what happened to Matney is still happening to good, major league-worthy players every year.

Another thing I learned about minor league baseball that first year: general managers get fired a lot. John Wallenstein, a 34-year-old White Sox fan who used to fill his car ash trays with stress-induced, chewed, wooden toothpicks, got the axe the day after the 1974 season. He was the bathwater and I was the baby. I was out of work, too.

LAFAYETTE, LA. 1975

The assistant general manager I worked for in Wichita, Bob Drew, was hired to be the general manager of a new Texas League team in Lafayette, Louisiana, and he invited me to the radio announcer. So I packed up the 1964 Buick LeSabre that I had bought for $200 when the old Triumph finally died and headed to Cajun Country with my wife and three kids.

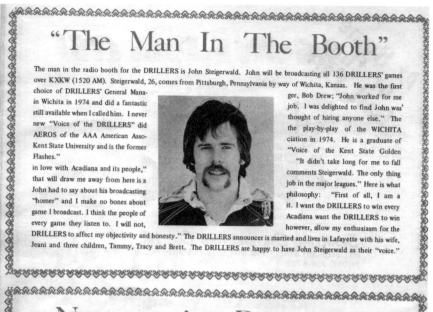
Back in 1975, I still thought it was a big deal to be described as "The Voice" of a baseball team. Even if it was for a team in Lafayette, Louisiana. I had dreams of being the man in a Major League booth some day. I would have been happy to shave the Fu Manchu.

My salary would be the same as it was in Wichita — $600 per month. My wife was promised a job working in the ticket booth on game nights and I could earn an extra $10 a game for sending game reports and box scores to the newspaper in Baton Rouge. My wife was also able to earn a few bucks by helping the GM's wife paint the ballpark.

The Lafayette Drillers, the "AA" affiliate of the San Francisco Giants, would be playing their home games in Clark Field. It had been used as a minor league ball park in the '50s but, since there had been no minor league baseball team in town since 1960, it had been converted into a high school football stadium.

To make what was a baseball park into a football stadium, they had installed bleachers that ran across the outfield. That made for an interesting baseball configuration. The fence down the leftfield line was 410 feet away. Straightaway centerfield was 345. The right field corner was about 300 feet and right center was something like 420.

It was exactly the kind of quirky thing that I loved about minor league baseball.

The team was owned by a young guy from Pittsburgh named Al Stuckman. His full name was Alan Rockwell Stuckman and, yes, it was *those* Rockwells. This guy had some bucks behind him. Al was a nice guy who had no idea how to run a baseball team and had to lean on Bob Drew for everything. Al was the kind of guy who would approve an expenditure of thousands of dollars one minute and then yell at Drew for giving a new season-ticket buyer a free souvenir miniature bat the next.

Al had to take medication for seizures and they made him drowsy. That made for some pretty bad advertising when the owner would be sound asleep in his third base box seat.

This was the Texas League and that meant we would be spending a lot of time riding on buses, so Drew and I decided it would be a good idea to secure one bus for the whole season and have it equipped with beds and a television. It was a good idea but the "beds" were more like luggage racks and the TV hardly ever worked.

We hired a bus driver for the season and he recruited the Drillers' manager, Denny Sommers, to spell him on the really long trips. Sommers was 35, had quite a temper and didn't like to lose. A couple of years later he would be expelled from the Southern League for punching out an umpire. (Another thing I loved about the minor leagues.)

When the team played the last game of a series, the bus would leave from the ball park and head for the next town on the schedule, which meant a lot of overnight bus rides. If that last game happened to be a loss or if it happened to be one of several losses in a row, Sommers would take it out on the bus.

I can remember many nights standing beside him as he sat behind the wheel with a big cigar sticking out of the side of his mouth and a really unhappy look on his face, driving along on a two-lane country highway.

The speedometer would be buried at 85.

I don't know why I felt the need to stand there. Maybe it was to make sure he didn't fall asleep. Fortunately, the Drillers were a good team, led by future major league star and major Pirate-killer, 19-year-old Jack Clark. Come to think of it, that good year that Jack had might have saved our lives.

The longest bus trip was between 20 and 24 hours from Alexandria, Louisiana, to El Paso, Texas. We only had to make that trip once and, believe me, once was enough.

Diablo Stadium in El Paso had something that you could only find in the minor leagues. The Diablos' public-address announcer provided running commentary throughout the game. When a Drillers pitcher was struggling, the announcer, whose name I don't recall, would say, over the loudspeaker, something like, "Hey, Sommers, how much more do you have to see of this guy? Stick a fork in him, he's done."

I remember the night he welcomed me to the game. In between innings, he said this to a ballpark full of people: "We'd like to welcome Drillers radio announcer John Steigerwald to the game tonight. He's sending the game back to Lafayette on KXKW." There was a smattering of polite applause and then he said this: "By the way, John, I just called your house and a man answered."

You're not going to get that at Yankee Stadium.

Something else you wouldn't get at Yankee Stadium is a championship baseball series being decided by a tug of war. If you look up the Texas League champion for 1975, you will see that there were co-champs, the Drillers and the Midland Cubs, who got a lot of help from a relief pitcher with a nasty split-finger fastball named Bruce Sutter. The Cubs were the Western Division champs and the Drillers had won the East. After four games the five-game series was tied 2-2. Lafayette had had several days of rain and Clark Field was mud soup. The final game was postponed a couple of times and the rain refused to let up, so Texas League President Bobby Bragan stepped in and declared co-champions. So the championship wasn't really decided by a tug of war, but Bragan asked both teams to participate in one so that the fans who had shown up for the rained-out game would get some kind of a show. Amazingly, the players went along with it. I don't remember who won.

Bob Drew did such a good job running the team in Lafayette that he was offered a job at a more established Texas League franchise in San Antonio and that meant I was moving again. Only it wouldn't be to San Antonio.

CHARLESTON, W.VA. 1976

The Pirates' stupid decision to fire Bob Prince after the 1975 season created an opening for an announcer in Charleston, West Virginia, where the Pirates had their Triple "A" affiliate. The Charleston announcer, Lanny Frattare, thanks to the exposure he got from Bob Prince allowing him to sit in on Pirates' broadcasts, had been hired to be Milo Hamilton's sidekick in Pittsburgh.

The team was named the Charlies after the team's really old owner, Charley Levine. One day, while I was looking for work, I was on the phone with Bill Turner, a guy who worked in the Pirates' minor league department, pumping him for any tips he might have about job openings. Bill said, "Carl Steinfeldt, the general manager in Charleston, is here in my office, why don't you talk to him."

I was a no-brainer pick for the job with my two years of experience and my knowledge of the Pirates. I got the usual $600 a month, plus a chance to earn a few bucks sending reports back to the Charleston Gazette from road games. My wife would work in the ticket booth on game nights.

The Charlies played their home games in Watt Powell Park, a beautiful old ballpark with big dimensions and railroad tracks running behind the right field wall.

They could have played their games in the Watt Powell parking lot. The attendance for the 1976 season was slightly over 70,000. Keep in mind that they played 70 home games and that there were two huge promotional nights that each drew over 4,000. That meant that, on most nights, there were about 800 people in the park.

It's not easy for a baseball announcer to sound good when a homerun call is followed by the kind of crowd noise you get at a church league softball game. Actually, there wasn't really any crowd noise. It was more like intermittent clapping.

Pretty depressing.

And it's not like the Charlies didn't have an interesting team.

The 1976 Charleston Charlies had a lot of future Major League players, including a few who spent quite a bit of time with the Pirates. Somehow, they managed to finish fourth in a six team league.

They had a future 20-game winner in the big leagues, Rick Langford, in the starting rotation and a guy who became a very good reliever in the majors and pitched beyond his 40th birthday, Doug Bair, in the bullpen.

Tony Armas, who became a 40-homerun hitter in the majors, was in center and Omar Moreno, who became the best base-stealer in the National League and helped the Pirates win a World Series in 1979, was in right. Everybody in Pittsburgh knows Moreno as a centerfielder but Armas had a better arm and that made Moreno a right fielder in Charleston.

Miguel Dilone — a switch hitter who never did much in the big leagues but went back and forth with Moreno for the International League lead in stolen bases and hit over .330 — was in left field. Ken Macha, a future, solid big-league utility man and now manager of the Milwaukee Brewers, was at third.

Craig Reynolds, who played almost 1,500 games in the majors, was at shortstop. The second baseman was a kid named Mike Richards who had a short career in the bigs. Mitchell Page, who came close to winning the AL Rookie of the Year Award the following year, when he hit 21 home runs and batted .307 for the Oakland A's, was the first baseman. Page, along with Langford and Bair, were part of the trade that sent Manny Sanguillen to Oakland for A's manager Chuck Tanner. The catcher was a 20-year-old kid named Steve Nicosia, who would platoon with Ed Ott on the Pirates' 1979 World Series winner.

Despite all that talent, the Charlies finished a distant fourth in a six-team league.

Maybe that's why the manager, Tim Murtaugh, never followed in his dad's footsteps to manage in the major leagues.

Not only did I have the absence of human beings in the ballpark to deal with during home games, but the cheap setup that I had in the radio booth picked up the paging system from the hospital that was down the street.

So, as I was trying to call the game, this is what I would hear in my head set and what I was pretty sure the listeners were hearing, too: "Paging Doctor Howard, Doctor Fine, Doctor Howard."

OK, the Three Stooges didn't work there, but they should have worked in the front office of the Charlies. They would have done a better job of putting people in the park.

When you're calling a game, you like to think that there are lots of people listening and that's what I always assumed, but looking back on it, if only 800 people were interested in seeing a team in person, how many would want to listen to their games on the radio?

I'm thinking that whoever was paging the doctors across the street had a bigger audience than I did.

I used to look forward to away games.

There were and still are some great minor league towns in the International League. Back then, the two best were Rochester (Orioles) and Syracuse (Yankees). There were always good crowds at those games.

The game I remember most from that 1976 season was played in Syracuse, where long-time Atlanta Braves manager Bobby Cox was the manager of the Chiefs. Miguel Dilone was the hottest hitter in the league at the time and he was even better than Moreno as a base-stealer. Dilone was a slap hitter who had been torturing International League pitchers for several weeks with bunt singles and balls slapped through the infield. Then, once he got on base, the torture really began. Nobody could throw him out trying to steal.

Cox devised a plan. He came up with "The Dilone Shift," which involved bringing one of the outfielders in to play directly behind second base. Dilone wasn't going to beat him with any bunt singles or Punch & Judy punches.

Dilone went 6-for-6.

Cox went on to become what is sure to be a Hall of Fame manager. Dilone played in the big leagues for about an hour and a half.

Despite those long trips the year before in the Texas League, it was in the International League where I took my most excruciating bus trips and they weren't very long ones, either.

The trip between Richmond and/or Tidewater (Norfolk) and Charleston was even worse than the trip from Alexandria, Louisiana, to El Paso, even though it was about one fourth as long.

Hot Time in the Old Town

John Steigerwald couldn't handle the heat yesterday afternoon at Parker Field, so the radio play-by-play announcer for the Charleston Charlies shed his shirt and _ for a breeze. If he had remained fully clothed, he probably would have gotten a bit hot under the collar as the Richmond Braves scored three runs in the bottom of the ninth inning to beat the Charlies, 6-5. (See Story, Page _

This picture that appeared in a Richmand, Va., newspaper on a hot day in the summer of 1976 is a good example of my approach to broadcasting. laid back, comfortable, and conversational.

The trip would always come after a night game, which meant that we would leave sometime around midnight. I had learned how to get something resembling sleep while sitting in a bus seat but I never slept a wink on this one.

On getaway night the players would bring a sixpack or two of beer on the bus with them. After they drank a beer, they would throw the can on the floor.

There are a lot of mountains between Richmond and Charleston and every time we would go up one, 50 cans would roll to the back of the bus. When we would go down, they would roll to the front. It was only a four or five hour ride as I recall, but nothing was worse than those cans rolling up and down the floor at 3 in the morning.

Of course, the sound of the cans was mixed with the sound of several boom boxes. Some playing R&B, some playing country and some playing whatever it was the Latin players liked to listen to.

As the season was coming to an end, it was obvious that the Charlies would be moving out of Charleston to play in the new ballpark in Columbus, Ohio. I thought I was ready for the big leagues and really didn't care, plus I also figured I had a pretty good shot at getting the job in Columbus.

Wrong on both counts.

I've mentioned that I learned a lot from the time I spent in the minor leagues and I learned one of my best lessons just before the end of that 1976 season.

I learned that major decisions are made in broadcasting by people who know nothing about what makes a good broadcaster.

Major League Baseball was expanding in 1977 and I thought I might have a shot at working for one of the expansion teams. I put a call into the Seattle Mariners and they told me to contact the radio station that would be carrying the games, so I did.

I don't remember the station but I'll never forget the conversation I had with whoever the creep was who was picking the announcers:

ME: Hi, my name's John Steigerwald and _____ at the Mariners told me to contact you about the radio announcer position.

CREEP: Hi, John, that position is still open and we're still accepting applications. Where are you working now?

ME: I'm doing play-by-play for the Pirates' Triple "A" team in Charleston, West Virginia.

CREEP: Sorry, John, we're looking for someone with major-market experience.

ME: You mean Major League Baseball experience?

CREEP: No. Not necessarily. We just want someone from a major market.

ME: I've been doing minor league play-by-play for the last three years, can I send you a tape?

CREEP: There's really no need to. As I said, we're looking for someone with experience in a major market.

(Now, I'm starting to get pissed thinking about the bus trips and the cans rolling up and down the aisle and the $600 a month and my wife working in the ticket booth and this jagoff dismissing three years of my life when, as far as he knows, I'm the next Jon Miller.)

ME: So, what you're saying is that you would rather hire a guy who's been sitting in front of a camera reading a Teleprompter in St. Louis for the last three years and has never called one inning of baseball play-by-play than even consider someone like me who has called 430 games over the last three years?

CREEP: (cockily) Yeah. That's right.

I hung up on him.

I wish I knew the guy's name because he's one of several people I would like to thank for saving me from a life of doing Major League Baseball play-by-play.

Another one is George Sisler, Jr., the GM in Columbus, who gave me no consideration for the radio job there, despite the fact that I had been highly recommended by everybody in Charleston. He hired a guy named John Gordon from Columbus, who called double plays "twin kills" and homeruns "round trippers." Gordon, of course, used those skills to get a job in the big leagues.

I sure as hell didn't think this at the time, but better him than me.

SHORT STOP
MR. BANKS

I learned a lot in the minor leagues, but what I learned went way beyond baseball. I lived in three very different parts of the country in three years and experienced three very different cultures.

Lafayette, Louisiana, is about as deep in the deep South as you can get and I may as well have had "YANKEE" tattooed on my forehead. It didn't take long for me to notice that every one of the Lafayette natives on the Lafayette Drillers' office staff matter-of-factly referred to the little black kids who hung around the office front door looking for free tickets or free souvenirs as "niggers."

I also noticed that when Ernie Banks came to town for a promotional appearance the same people all referred to him as "Mister Banks."

It didn't take long for Ernie, one of the nicest guys in sports history, to be reminded that he was in the deep South.

A reporter named Guy Rials was in the Drillers office to do a one-on-one interview with Banks for the local paper and he found out that Banks was an avid golfer.

Rials was also the local golf writer and he started making calls to some of his friends at the better golf courses in the area. As I watched him making the calls I could see that he was getting more and more pissed off.

Then I heard him say, "Well if you have to ask, never mind."

Rials couldn't find a golf course that would allow "Mister Banks" to play.

I begged the general manager, Bob Drew to let me rip them all on the air that night and he said, "Let's wait." When there were only a few games left in the season, he gave me the go ahead.

I told the Banks story on the air and then said, "What this place needs is an airlift to drop a few thousand calendars with the century circled."

Apparently, the fine citizens of Cajun Country didn't take too kindly to a Yankee scolding them on the radio and lots of sponsors called Drew and told him to get rid of the radio announcer.

Drew left after the season to take a job in San Antonio. For some reason, the new Drillers GM thought it would be a good idea to find a new radio announcer and I was on my way to Wild 'n' Wonderful West Virginia. I learned that, while letting it rip on the radio may feel good at the time, it can have life-altering consequences.

CHAPTER 12

SHORT STOP
PITCHING RACISM

IT'S Spring, 1975 and I'm sitting in the Clark Field radio booth preparing to call a Lafayette Drillers' game. Out on the field, just behind the pitcher's mound I can see the Giants' roving minor league pitching instructor surrounded by several pitchers who are at least trying to look interested. As I'm watching this I can't help but wonder how the two black pitchers in the group could expect to get a fair evaluation when the coach sent his report back to the parent club. And I'm wondering how many black pitchers, who were only slightly better than white pitchers, might have been kept in the minor leagues because of the coach's evaluations, while the slightly or maybe not so slightly less talented white guys were promoted. I had good reason to wonder. Earlier that day I was standing in the Drillers' office with the assistant general manager, Danny Adams. We happened to be standing in front of a picture that was hanging in every baseball office in North America that Spring—the picture of Henry Aaron hitting his 715th homerun the year before. The coach strolled through the front door, walked up to us and, under his breath, offered this brilliant commentary, "Somebody should have taken a high powered rifle and shot that fucking nigger in the head." He later went on to become a major league pitching coach with the Giants, Mariners, Royals and Rockies. I always wondered if any of the black pitchers on his staff ever got the idea that they were being treated a little differently. Because of that incident, to this day, I never dismiss any player's claim that he is being treated differently because he's black.

(I had planned to reveal the name of the coach but changed my mind. I decided to give him the benefit of the doubt and assume that he has evolved from that position. I guess you could do a little research and find out his name. I'll leave that up to you.)

CHAPTER 13

SHORT STOP
SATCH

ONE day in 1974, early in my tenure as the radio voice of the Wichita Aeros, I was sitting in the Aeros' Lawrence Stadium office. I performed my main duties at night from 7 o'clock until about 10 o'clock, but I was also expected to make myself useful during the day by hanging out in the Aeros' outer office taking care of people who came in off the street looking to buy tickets or get information.

I remember it being a rainy day and, as I sat there working on the team stats — another one of my official duties — a 60ish or 70ish black man came literally shuffling in the door. I swear he was wearing bedroom slippers.

Just as I was about to give him my best "Can I help you, sir?" the general manager, John Wallenstein, opened the door to his office and called out, "Hi, Satch."

Then I was introduced to Satchel Page, one of the most colorful characters in baseball history.

And, some say, the best pitcher — ever.

I don't know why I hadn't been told that Satchel Page would be dropping by. Maybe because they were afraid a wide-eyed, 25-year-old kid would make an idiot of himself.

I tried not to.

After a few minutes of small talk, my boss told me that my job that day was going to be driving Satch around Wichita to various media outlets so that he could promote his upcoming appearance at Lawrence Stadium.

I wish I had kept a tape recorder running because I'm sure I could have devoted a lot more space in this book to all the great things that Page told me during the few hours that I spent with him. I hate to admit it but I don't remember any one thing that he said except this:

When I asked if those great Negro League teams from the '30s and '40s were really as good or better than the great major league teams from that era, including the Yankees, he said, "Ain't no maybe so about it."

That's all I remember from my day with the great Satchel Page, but it's enough for me. I've repeated that quote a million times myself since then and those few hours that I spent with him were exactly why I was willing to work in a godforsaken place like Wichita, Kansas, for $600 a month.

CHAPTER 14

SHORT STOP
THE (REALLY) OLD
LEFTHANDER

I crossed paths with another one of baseball's legendary figures when Carl Hubbell showed up in Lafayette, Louisiana, in the summer of 1975.

Hubbell was a left-handed screwball pitcher who won 253 games in 16 seasons with the New York Giants but achieved baseball immortality when, in the second All-Star Game in 1934, he struck out Babe Ruth, Lou Gehrig, Jimmy Foxx, Al Simmons and Joe Cronin in succession.

The Lafayette Drillers, the team that was paying me to do the play-by-play of their games on the radio, were the Giants' Double "A" affiliate and Hubbell was one of their roving minor league pitching coaches.

Denny Sommers, the Drillers manager, when he heard that Hubbell was coming to town, told me to make sure that I checked out Hubbell's left arm. He said that because of all those screwballs that he threw, Hubbell's left arm hung with the palm of his left hand facing out. A screwball, in case you didn't know, requires the opposite wrist action from a curveball.

Hubbell was 72 and looked like he was 92, but that could have been because I was only 27 and anybody over 60 looked ancient to me. Although, I do think that 72 was a lot older in 1975 than it is in 2010.

I was introduced to Hubbell when he showed up at the Drillers' office and I couldn't wait to check out that left arm. As soon as he turned and walked away I saw that Denny was right.

His left arm looked like it was screwed on wrong.

I have to admit I was pretty impressed with myself for having hung out with Carl Hubbell and I was sure that the Drillers' pitchers would be even more impressed to know that they were going to be observed and advised by a living legend.

Prior to the game, Hubbell was introduced to the crowd and a big deal was made about Lafayette being fortunate enough to be visited by a baseball immortal.

A few innings into the game I said, "If you're just tuning in, we're happy to have a baseball legend with us here at Clark Field. Carl Hubbell, the Giants' roving pitching instructor and Hall of Famer, is here to observe the Drillers pitchers for a few days. He's sitting behind home plate."

As I was saying that I glanced down to where Hubbell was sitting and noticed that he was sound asleep.

Meeting and spending time with baeball immortals like Bob Feller,
Satchel page, and Carl Hubbell made life in the minor leagues inter-
esting and I didn't just get to meet them. I got to pick their brains.
Feller was a man of many politically incorrect opinions and wasn't
shy about expressing them.

CHAPTER 15

KILL THE PERSON

JUST this morning I saw a report on Fox News about a high school kid who was suspended for six weeks for bringing a two-inch penknife to school. The best part of the story was that the knife was never brought into the school building. Somehow, word got out that he had the deadly weapon in the glove compartment of his car. Of course, the kid was a real pain in the ass — a real problem child.

He was the son of a police chief who had never been in trouble and his biggest worry after the suspension was whether it would affect his ability to get an appointment to West Point. This was coupled with a story about a six-year-old who was suspended for bringing a Cub Scout mess kit to school. This little menace was actually brandishing the foldout knife, fork and spoon before the authorities stepped in and saved the lives of hundreds of innocent children.

What the hell is going on in school these days?

I know we've had some horrific shooting incidents, but are our kids supposed to have confidence in adults who are afraid of Cub Scout cutlery? A large part of it is a result of the media hysteria surrounding the school shootings and some of the precautions are legitimate, but I blame most of the stupidity on women.

OK, wait. Maybe that's not fair.

Effeminate men are to blame, too.

Do a survey of your local elementary school and check out the ratio of female to male teachers. I'll bet it's around 10-1.

I'm sure you've heard the stories about schools in various parts of the country banning tag. Is there a real man, who doesn't sit down to pee, who would ever think about banning tag?

I had radio guests trying to defend this stupidity by blaming it on the fear of a lawsuit and that may be a legitimate concern. But no real man would sue a school over his son or daughter falling down and going boom during a game of tag. So, it still comes back to a woman or an effeminate man.

The scary thing is that we're going to have a generation of adult males who were feminized by this nonsense and lots of them will think it's normal to think of tag as a dangerous game.

When I was roaming the playgrounds at St. Bernard and Our Lady of Grace Catholic grade schools in the late '50s and early '60s, we played a game called "Kill the Man."

Imagine trying to get away with that today.

A kid would be expelled from school just for bringing a videogame with a name like that to school.

Now, if the playground game were allowed, a kid might get away with playing "Kill the *Person*." Forget kill the *man*.

"Kill the Man" was a pretty simple game. It required a small ball that bounced, a playground and lots of 10- to 13-year-old boys who had been cooped up in a building looking at nuns for three hours.

There were no teams.

It was every man for himself.

Sorry, girls.

The game began when the owner of the ball threw it straight up as high as he could. Whoever caught it was "The Man" and everybody tried to kill him. Not literally, of course, but some sort of injury was always a possibility.

The Man ran with the ball until he was tackled or, in order to avoid being swarmed under by Sister Cecelia's entire sixth grade class, he threw it away to be picked up by the next Man.

There was no scoring.

It was pure, unadulterated, unorganized mayhem.

You know, *fun*.

To this day, I'm not sure how a winner was declared. I think the Man in possession of the ball when the school bell rang was the winner. Keep in mind that this was played on asphalt and boys were not allowed to wear jeans to school. Lots of kids wore khakis with patches on the knees. Even a really good "Kill the Man" player could tear up a pair of pants a week.

There were no lawsuits that I can recall.

I'm sure at both of my grade schools, St. Bernard and Our Lady of Grace, there were many more female teachers than male because we were taught by nuns.

The difference, of course, was that the nuns were not known for their ability to evaluate a conflict and then work to resolve it without anyone's self-esteem being damaged.

They were known mostly for beating the shit out of any kid who got out-of-line.

Make that any *boy* who got out-of-line. Girls rarely got out-of-line. It was much more fun for them to watch the boys get slapped around. I went to St. Bernard in Mt. Lebanon from the first to the fifth grade and there were several male teachers, but they were referred to as "coaches." Football was very important at St. Bernard. The team went something like 13 years without losing a game. I'm going to take a wild guess and say that there were no rules about everybody getting a chance to play in a game. If you were good enough, you got playing time. If you weren't, you didn't. Today, that alone would get everybody fired or sued or both.

Maybe I missed it but, over the years, I never noticed an alarming number of psychopathic killers produced by the good Sisters of St. Joseph at St. Bernard. The pastor, Father Lonergan, was a huge fan of Notre Dame football and managed to work a Fighting Irish reference into almost every sermon.

Something else he tried to work into as many sermons as possible: How much he hated the Boy Scouts. He made fun of their shorts and called them sissies and said they should cut out the crap and play football.

A pastor who tried that today would get a call from the Pope.

We all know that the concept of pick-up games for kids died a long, long time ago. Now, everything is organized, including which mom will be in charge of the snacks.

St. Bernard had an intramural program that could only exist at a school where men were calling the shots.

It began with the fourth graders. The teacher's only involvement was overseeing the election of the team captain. Imagine this happening today: 25 nine-year old boys (there were about 50 kids in each home room) elect the captain of their softball team. The captain is in charge of picking the starting lineup and making the batting order. The teacher has no input. The parents have nothing to say and never show up for a game. The schedule and standings are printed in the church bulletin every Sunday. There were five home rooms in each grade. I was captain of the team from 4-1. The other fourth grade teams were 4-2, 4-3, 4-4 and 4-5. I can remember thinking it was pretty cool seeing those standings in the church bulletin.

The only adult supervision on game day was when the male teacher or "coach" picked the umpires from a group of fourth-graders whose teams were off that day. Again, try to picture this happening today. No snack moms hanging around. A fourth-grader calling balls and strikes and three more fourth-graders working the bases. We used a mush ball and there were no gloves. We played on asphalt and if the situation called for it, we slid. Whoever was leading when the bell rang was the winner.

Football was the same. Captains set the lineups, other fourth-graders worked as officials.

I don't remember major arguments and I know there weren't any lawsuits. I also know that if girls had been allowed to play, it wouldn't have lasted 15 minutes.

I'll tell you a little secret and I hope the statute of limitations protects these guys, but the coaches/teachers at St. Bernard were also known to — are you ready? — organize snowball fights! That's right. These barbarians would actually put the fourth-graders behind the mounds made by the snowplows and have the kids make a large supply of snowballs and then they would order the fifth-graders to attack. If someone tried that today, it would end up on somebody's cell phone, then on YouTube and Bill O'Reilly would be debating it on Fox News with a child psychologist (most likely a woman) who would be demanding that the evil men be charged with child abuse and sent to prison.

Amazingly enough, in the course of your life, you have probably encountered a St. Bernard Snowball Wars survivor and not been aware. They hide their scars — including the emotional ones — well.

CHAPTER 16

THE PIRATES ARE COMING, TRA-LA, TRA-LA

MILO Hamilton smoked a pipe.

That's pretty much all you need to know about him and why he was a dismal failure in Pittsburgh when he tried to follow Bob Prince's act as Voice of the Pirates.

In what may be the worst public relations/marketing move in the history of North American sports, KDKA and the Pirates fired Prince and his partner, Nellie King, after the 1975 season. Joe L. Brown, the Pirates General Manager and KDKA GM Ed Wallace were fed up with Prince and they most likely had plenty of legitimate gripes.

"The Gunner" had gotten somewhat out of control both on the air and off and had been warned many times.

He thought he was bigger than the job.

Turns out he was.

The fans couldn't send e-mails back then, but they could make phone calls and send letters and they did that by the thousands.

There was a parade to protest the firings and to put pressure on both the Pirates and KDKA to change their minds.

Neither would budge. Nor would either of them take full responsibility for the firing. It was a joint effort but it could not have happened without the Pirates' consent.

It couldn't have come at a worse time for the Pirates.

The Gunner with me and Paul on Paul's wedding day.

The Steelers were about to win their second Super Bowl and were about to take over from the Pirates as the most popular team in town. Notice I said about to. I know it's hard for anybody under the age of 50 to imagine, but, until that second Super Bowl win, the Pirates were the most popular and most important team in town, even if their attendance figures didn't reflect that.

Three Rivers Stadium was a great football stadium but it was an absolutely hideous place for baseball. Bob Prince was a Pittsburgh original and

85

an icon. When he was removed from the picture, Myron Cope was there to fill the void.

The Pirates had won division titles in 1970, '71, '72, '74 and '75, with a World Series win in '71 and, in the fall of 1975, they were a much more successful team than the Steelers. In fact, it wasn't even close.

Pirates fans had demonstrated a dislike for Three Rivers Stadium almost immediately. Twenty thousand felt like a big crowd at Forbes Field. (As it does at PNC Park, which is why PNC Park only has 36,000 seats.) The same crowd at Three Rivers made you wonder where everybody was.

Fifteen thousand at Three Rivers Stadium created a traffic jam that was as bad or worse than rush hour traffic.

So, at just about the exact moment when the Pirates were about to be passed in popularity by the Steelers, they fired a guy who was as popular as any player who ever wore a Pirates uniform.

And they replaced him with a nerd who smoked a pipe.

I remember seeing a skit on "Saturday Night Live" back then that was a takeoff on the warning signs for cancer. They were warning signs that might indicate that you were pretentious.

Smoking a pipe was at the top of the list.

Bob Prince was a man's man who smoked Pall Mall's and drank screw drivers.

Milo smoked a pipe.

Prince also was probably more involved in the promotion of charitable causes than anybody in the history of the city. And he was always doing little things that endeared him to people.

Like the time he told everybody at KDKA-TV to hold off on buying their Thanksgiving turkeys and then showed up at the station a few days before the holiday with a truckload of them.

Radio Rich, an orphan who was employed by Prince to be a radio booth gopher, became a fixture in Pittsburgh press boxes and was able to earn a living despite his limited abilities and lack of any social skills. The Gunner treated him like a son. He even made Rich famous by talking about him on the radio all the time. The Gunner turned a lonely nobody into a somebody just because he could.

Victor Vrable, long time floor director at KDKA-TV was working as a broadcast booth gopher for Prince in the early '60s. After every game, Prince would drive him to his bus stop so he could get home to Clairton.

Every once in a while, they would pop into a bar near the bus stop. One night, Vrable realized that he had just missed the last bus. Prince had Vrable get in his car and he sped up Route 51 until he caught up to the bus. When the bus stopped, Prince pulled his car in front of it and jumped out. The bus driver was a little alarmed until he saw who it was.

Prince said, "You're this kid's last bus, sorry about pulling in front of you there." The driver told Prince not to worry about it and went on his way. But he didn't drop Vrable at his usual stop. He took him to his front door. That's the kind affection people had for Prince.

Not long after that, Prince asked Vrable why he didn't have a car. Vrable, who was only 20 years old at the time, said that he couldn't afford one. So, Prince said, "Go find a car and I'll buy it for you." Vrable found himself a good used car for $600. The Gunner wrote the check and told Vrable that he could give him $5 a week to pay him back.

After a few months of making the payments, Prince returned all the money that Vrable had given him and said, "Don't worry about it, kid."

You could fill a book with stories like that. Bob Prince was truly a Pittsburgh original.

Did I mention that Milo smoked a pipe?

Lanny Frattare, who was cut from the same broadcasting mold as Milo —lots of stats and a mellifluous voice — was hired to be his sidekick. (I took Lanny's place doing radio play-by-play in Charleston, West Virginia, for the Pirates AAA team.)

The night of Milo's and Lanny's first game, I asked a friend of mine, who was a huge fan of Bob Prince, what he thought.

"They sound like they're describing brain surgery." Another guy said they sounded like they were describing a state funeral.

Neither Milo nor Lanny sounded that bad in his own right.

They sounded that bad in comparison to Bob Prince.

They never had a chance.

Vince Leonard, a radio/TV critic for the Post-Gazette, ripped them and the talk shows were bombarded with people saying they'll never listen to another game unless Bob Prince is brought back.

Lots of people who used to listen to Prince and his partner Nellie King religiously started tuning into Myron Cope's talk show at 7 p.m. Myron was on his way to becoming a legend almost as large as Prince.

Milo was on his way out of town.

It took five years only because of the Pirates' and KDKA's stupidity.

Keep in mind that the Steelers had what may have been their best team ever in 1976 and were probably on their way to their third consecutive Super Bowl if not for injuries to Rocky Bleier and Franco Harris in a blowout playoff win over the Colts.

Pitt went undefeated and won the Mythical National Championship and Tony Dorsett won the Heisman Trophy. Other than that, the Pirates had no competition for attention in their first year without a guy who was as popular as any player in their history.

You could say that 1976 was the year that Pittsburgh went from being a baseball town to a football town. Bob Prince in the radio booth couldn't have stopped that from happening, but he could have slowed down the process.

The stupidity of Major League Baseball's revenue structure has made the Pirates irrelevant since 1993, but, even without that, the Pirates would still be paying the price for firing "The Gunner."

When Milo was finally run out of town, Bob Smizik wrote in the Pittsburgh Press that he had gotten a raw deal and was treated unfairly by the fans.

He also dismissed the claims that Prince's firing had hurt attendance and said that criticizing Milo for his clichés was holding him to a double standard because Prince had plenty of them, too.

Of course Prince's clichés weren't cliché's. They were his sayings:

"Kiss it goodbye."

"Bug loose on the rug."

"We need a Hoover. (That was his way of saying that the Pirates needed a double play. Westinghouse, the corporate owner of KDKA, told him to stop using that one because Hoover was a competitor.)

"Foul by a gnat's eyelash."

"Home run in an elevator shaft."

Those were Prince originals.

Here are some of Milo's greatest hits:

"Round tripper."

"Twin killing."

"Holy Toledo."

(I remember hearing Milo being interviewed shortly after he was hired and he was asked by a caller if he had any catch phrases that the fans should look for. Milo said, "When I get really excited, I say 'Holy Toledo.'" I knew he was toast.)

When he got really crazy and came up with a Milo-ism, he laid this one on Pirates fans:

"The Pirates are coming tra-la, tra-la."

There's a guy with his finger on the pulse of his listeners.

I'll be that got the guys drinking boilermakers in Bloomfield whipped into a frenzy.

It was absurd to suggest that the radio announcer had nothing to do with attendance. It's hard to imagine now, but, in 1975, the Pirates televised 30 of their games, all on the road. Now, there are fewer than 15 games that are *not* on television. That means that, for 132 games a year, Pirates fans' only impression of the Pirates came from what they heard on the radio. Bob Prince would do six innings per game, King would do the middle three.

I know that my early love for the Pirates and baseball was a direct result of listening to Bob Prince on the radio and I know that most of my friends felt the same way. Multiply that by the tens of thousands and then tell me that removing that ingredient from the equation wouldn't affect attendance and the Pirates' standing among sports fans in the long run.

Any time someone from the Pirates' front office would show up on a talk show, it was inevitable that a caller would beg him to bring back "The Gunner." The answer was always, "We think Milo and Lanny are doing a fine job."

It was a perfect example of the Pirates' cluelessness.

They kept saying "we" and never realized that it wasn't "we" who they were trying to please and it wasn't "we" who they were trying to get to buy tickets.

It was "they."

"They" were the fans and "they" were still pissed off and staying away in droves.

People from the Pirates' front office were always telling me that Prince never had any effect on attendance. I always disagreed and said that it was the long-term effect that would hurt them.

Also, there were already questions about attendance in 1975. Only an idiot would think firing a guy with Prince's clout while they were trying to solve an attendance problem was a good idea.

Then, in 1985, when he was dying of cancer, Prince made a return to the booth. The attendance that night was twice what it normally was and, when he waved to the crowd from the radio booth, he got a standing ovation that was as wild, loud and long as any player had ever gotten at Three Rivers Stadium.

I was there that night and when the cheering stopped, I went directly to where a Pirates front-office official was sitting in the press box and I said, "And you guys are going to tell me that that ingredient missing for the last 10 years hasn't hurt your attendance?"

There was nothing he could say.

Pirates fans were never able to relate to Milo and he resented that and was never able to relate to the fans. I think he resented them for liking Prince so much.

I remember one incident a few years into Milo's tenure. He was standing up in the KDKA radio booth, which, at that time, was just above the first level of seats behind home plate. Some college-aged guys spotted him and started chanting, "Milo, Milo, Milo." Milo, took a puff on his pipe and walked over to the railing, probably thinking that he should acknowledge these fans who were smart enough to recognize his greatness. He leaned over the railing and gave them a "pope wave" — the kind that the pope makes when he's acknowledging the throngs below his window at the Vatican.

The three guys, in unison, yelled out, "Give us a stat."

Milo slinked back into the booth.

Both Milo and Lanny Frattare really liked stats.

They liked to tell you what a guy was hitting in the series and when a player hit a double, they liked to tell you how many he had for the season. They would also tell you when a guy was on a three-game "hitting streak."

Prince went out of his way to avoid stats.

He would take the handout that the Pirates gave to every media person covering the game and that would be all that he needed.

He wanted to know a hitter's batting average, home runs and RBIs and he wanted the pitcher's record and ERA.

Milo would describe a double by Dale Berra and then say, "That's his eighth double of the year."

Who cares?

Unless he's leading the league in doubles or is about to set some kind of record for doubles, does it matter?

Prince avoided stats because *anybody* can throw out a stat. He was more interested in telling stories. The kind you get from hanging around batting cages for 30 years. Ask people old enough to remember when Prince called Pirates games and they'll tell you how much they enjoyed rain delays because of the stories and the interviews that Prince would get with visiting writers, scouts and front-office people.

Prince was so popular in the baseball culture that he would always get the big names to sit in with him during his broadcasts.

Milo considered interesting baseball characters a distraction.

If he had Stan Musial in the booth with him, he might forget to tell you how many doubles Dale Berra had.

If you can find a tape of the series clinching game in the 1979 NLCS, you can hear Milo calling the last out: "Here's the windup and the pitch, strike three swinging. That's Blyleven's 10th strikeout of the game and the Pirates win the pennant."

He couldn't help himself. Milo had to tell you that Blyleven had 10 strikeouts *before* he mentioned that they had won the pennant.

"The Gunner" would have said, "Here's the two-two pitch, struck him out swinging. The Pirates win the pennant." Then, he would have shut up and let the crowd go for 20 or 30 seconds before saying another word.

Unfortunately for the planet Earth, Milo's voice will be forever linked to Henry Aaron's 715th home run in 1974.

He was doing the play-by-play for the Braves and he actually made his lowly sidekick, Ernie Johnson, turn the mic over to him for every one of Aaron's at bats from home run 713 on. Milo said that he thought for months about what he would say on Number 715.

He did the radio call and screamed his lungs out while Aaron circled the bases and said, among other things, "There's a new home run king and his name is Henry Aaron."

Here's how Prince would have called it.

"Here's the pitch. Long drive deep to left. Kiss it goodbye. Number 715."

Then, he would have shut up and all that would have been heard was crowd noise. "The Gunner" gave his audience more credit and realized he didn't have to be part of the show. He would have known that everybody listening was aware of the importance and historical significance of number 715.

As much of a showman as Prince was, he always knew that nothing he could say was more exciting than 40,000 or 50,000 people screaming.

In October of 1979, I was minding my own business waiting at the gate to board the Pirates charter to Baltimore for the World Series. Milo walked up to me and said (in his deepest "The Pirates are coming, tra-la, tra-la" voice), "Hey, Steigerwald, when you've been doing this for 23 years, let me know." I said, "OK, Milo, I'll keep you in mind."

Milo was telling me that he was a grizzled veteran of the radio booth and I was a young punk.

Right on both counts.

He could have done Pirates play-by-play for 123 years and never created one new Pirates fan.

(After Milo was fired by the Cubs in 1985, baseball stats guru Bill James criticized the Chicago media for criticizing the Cubs. He said Milo "broadcasts games in a tone that would be more appropriate for a man reviewing a loan application."

And James is a guy who owes his very existence to stats.

I guess, in the interest of full disclosure, I should tell you about my first meeting with Milo. It might explain why I was never a big fan of his and why I was happy to see him fail.

It was the summer of 1976 and I was doing the play-by-play of the Charleston (W.Va.) Charlies, the Pirates' Triple "A" affiliate. For some reason, we had an off day on a Sunday and I decided to get a press pass and go to a Pirates game. I was coming out of the press box when I saw Milo standing outside the Pirates radio booth by himself, looking out at the Pirates taking batting practice.

I politely introduced myself and said I was the play-by-play announcer in Charleston. I didn't expect Milo to be impressed and I didn't expect him to do what Bob Prince had done for Lanny Frattare and invite me to sit in with him on the Pirates broadcast. I did think he might be a little interested in talking to me if, for no other reason, than to ask me how Omar Moreno, Craig Reynolds, Tony Armas, Steve Nicosia and Rick Langford were doing. After, all, I was armed with some information about prospects that would be interesting to Pirates listeners.

I even had stats, for God's sake.

Milo turned and put out his hand, we shook and he said (in the Milo "tra-la, tra-la" voice, of course), "Nice to see ya.'"

It was the old "Nice to see ya' but it's really not nice to see ya and would ya please get out of here and let me smoke my pipe" greeting.

He turned away immediately.

I got the message.

I got to know Bob Prince pretty well and I can guarantee you that he would have, at the very least, shown a genuine interest in the Pirates triple "A" announcer, whoever it was. Lanny Frattare called Pirates games for 30 years because of the times that "The Gunner" let him call a few innings of a Pirates game.

I had paid a visit to the Pirates' press box in 1975 after finishing a season of doing the play-by-play for the Giants double "A" team in Lafayette, La. Prince was actually not working that day because of a family event but Nellie King heard that I was there and invited me to sit in with him for an inning or two.

The warmth that Milo showed me that day in 1976 came through on his broadcasts. That's why there probably weren't 10 letters mailed or phone calls made to protest when he was finally and deservedly run out of town.

WHILE WE'RE ON THE SUBJECT

Listening to Bob Prince for the first 27 years of my life spoiled me. I can remember listening to the Cleveland Indians broadcasts when I was in college and feeling sorry for the fans who had to listen to Dave Martin (who later replaced Milo in Pittsburgh and lasted about an hour and a half before he was on his way out of town) because he was so boring and phony sounding.

He had that "baseball announcer's" voice.

After listening to "The Gunner," the rest of them all sounded the same. When I was doing the games in Charleston, a young fan in Syracuse asked me for a tape of one of my broadcasts. He was a radio geek and he had tapes of just about every major league announcer and he had been collecting tapes from the visiting minor league guys. I made a deal with him. I told him I would give him a tape of my broadcast if he would put together a tape with as many announcers as possible on it. I thought it would be a great way to prove my point that virtually all baseball announcers sounded the same.

He gave me the tape and it proved my point way beyond my wildest imagination. It was stunning how much they all sounded alike.

Same phony voice.

Same clichés.

I went out of my way not to have a "baseball announcer's voice" and I refused to ever refer to a home run as a "round tripper," a double as a "two-bagger" or a double play as a "twin killing."

It was a sure-fire plan to keep me out of the big leagues.

But the kid's tape wasn't my best example.

That happened early in my first season as the voice of the Wichita Aeros, the Cubs' triple "A" farm team. In 1974 I had replaced a guy, Larry Calton, who had been hired to do games for the Minnesota Twins and for the first two months on the job, all I heard was how great he was.

Calton was a former player who used to make his teammates laugh with his Harry Caray impersonations. He turned that into a job in Wichita, where he continued to imitate Caray in every way.

It's about two weeks into the Aeros' season and I'm in Wichita sitting in the Lawrence Stadium office after calling a game. The Aeros General Manager, John Wallenstein, and his assistant, Bob Drew, are listening to the Twins game on WHO out of Des Moines, Iowa.

Wallenstein says, "That's Larry, he sounds good."

Drew says, "No that's Herb Carneal."

Wallenstein says, "No, listen, that's Larry."

Drew's wife came in and Drew says, "Hey, Marge, isn't that Larry?"

She wasn't sure but she guessed that it was.

This is the guy they had been telling me was so great and they listened to him for five minutes and couldn't tell if it was Calton or his broadcast partner?

I didn't say a word. I just sat there knowing that they had just had an argument that could never have occurred in Pittsburgh when Bob Prince was calling the games.

One word out of *his* mouth and you knew.

CHAPTER 17

SHORT STOP
PISSING IN SINKS

I wouldn't be writing this sentence if not for Bob Prince because I wouldn't be writing a book if not for him. Bob Prince is why I got into sports-casting. I started out with the idea that I wanted to be a Major League Baseball announcer because of all those days and nights listening to "The Gunner" on the radio when I was a kid. So, it was no small thrill for me to be working with him in October of 1979 at the World Series.

Prince had been fired in 1975 by the Pirates and KDKA in what is still the worst PR move in Pittsburgh sports history and he was doing free-lance work. ABC and Channel 4 were carrying the World Series and Prince was hired to work with me and Bill Hillgrove to co-host the pre-game shows.

WTAE had paid a family, whose front porch provided a great view of Memorial Stadium, for the use of their home on game nights in Baltimore. I was sitting between Hillgrove and Prince on a couch in the living room of our rented house watching TV. After a few minutes, Prince got up from the couch and went upstairs and then came back and took his seat on the couch.

And then the guy I grew up listening to, the guy who used to say "Kiss it good-bye" to home runs and "Hello" to all the shut-ins said this:

"I just pissed in their sink."

Hillgrove and I, by this time, had already worked with The Gunner" for several days and had learned not to be shocked by anything that came out of his mouth, but that one set us back a bit.

Then "The Gunner" said, " I always piss in the sink. Do you know how much water is wasted when you flush a toilet? Urine is clean. I just turn on the faucet, piss in the sink and wash it down the drain. It's not a big deal."

Of course, by this time, Hillgrove and I are falling off the couch.

"The Gunner" wasn't done.

He very calmly and matter-of-factly said, "I pissed in (Pirates owner) John Galbreath's sink."

Hillgrove and I are dying.

"The Gunner" looks up at the ceiling trying to remember and then he says:

"I pissed in Bing Crosby's sink."

"I pissed in the sink at the American Embassy in Paris."

"I pissed in the sink at the White House."

There's no moral to the story. It's just one of those stories that at some point had to be made public and I decided that 30 years in the vault was long enough.

Now the world knows that Bob Prince not only enriched the lives of millions of people in Western Pennsylvania with his one-of-a kind baseball descriptions and his unending charitable work. But that he also was a conservationist who was way ahead of his time. What a guy.

CHAPTER 18

SPEAKING OF SPORTS

NOBODY influenced me more or made me want to be a sportscaster more than Bob Prince, but Howard Cosell wasn't a distant second.

Most people were first introduced to Cosell when he showed up in the ABC booth for "Monday Night Football" in 1970. Hard-core sports fans were aware of him earlier because of his work covering boxing for ABC and, of course, his association with Muhammad Ali.

I liked him long before he was cool.

I used to listen to him on KQV radio in the early-to-mid-Sixties. He was a commentator who actually had something to say and he said it in his own voice. He didn't have one of those phony radio voices that have always made me want to puke.

I can still hear Howard saying this on April 4, 1962, the day after Benny "The Kid" Paret died from injuries suffered in a March 24 nationally televised fight with Emile Griffith. (Instruct your brain to do its best Howard Cosell imitation when you read this. It'll work much better.)

"Hello again, everyone. This is Howard Cosell speaking of sports. In boxing, 'The Kid' is dead.

"Back in 60 seconds."

I don't remember what he said after the commercial but I'm sure it knocked my socks off. Years later I read in a TV Guide story about Cosell that he almost never wrote out his 60-second radio commentaries. He did them off the top of his head and was always able to wrap it up in a perfectly neat package just as the second hand was crossing the 12.

Live.

That qualifies him for "From Another Planet" status.

If I'm not mistaken, the TV Guide writer had sat in the studio and watched Cosell do a spectacular commentary on the death of Vince Lombardi without a script.

I had two close encounters with Howard. The first one was at the 1979 World Series. I spent the entire series co-hosting pre-game shows on WTAE-TV with Bob Prince and it was a pretty big deal when Prince introduced me to Howard, who was working the series for ABC. We spent a good part of a morning hanging with the Gunner and Howard in the lobby of the Cross Keys Hotel outside of Baltimore. Bill Hillgrove, who was also co-hosting the pre-game shows, had set up an interview with Cosell to use on the next show. The subject would be one of Howard's favorites: "The Jockocracy." Howard, who worked with two ex-jocks in the "Monday Night Football" booth and with at least one in the World Series booth, had become very outspoken about the increasing number of ex-athletes passing themselves off as journalists.

That's perfect Howard Cosell.

Most guys in his position would never have the balls to take that stance. Actually, nobody in his position ever had and, as far as I know, ever has.

I stood behind the camera as Bill sat with Howard on a couch to do the interview. Here's how the interview went:

HILLGROVE: Howard, speak, if you will, about what you call "The Jockocracy."

COSELL : "Blah, blah, blah..."

I don't remember a thing he said. I just know that he went on for at least four minutes with an answer that sounded like it was being read from a written page. Everybody who was paying attention stood there with their mouths open. He made perfect sense. There were dramatic pauses, inflections and changes in volume. He wrapped it up perfectly and sat back waiting for the next question.

There was no next question.

Bill Hillgrove just threw his head back, flipped the microphone and said, "That was unbelievable."

The interview was over. There was nothing left for anyone to say. I wish I had the tape. I'm sure it still exists somewhere in the bowels of WTAE-TV.

A few minutes later, I was standing in the lobby with Cosell and Bob Prince and an African-American busboy sheepishly approached Cosell and asked for an autograph. Howard gave the kid a look and, in his perfect Howard Cosell voice, said, "I don't normally sign for blacks." Then he laughed, took the kids pen and paper and signed. He made sure the kid knew that he was kidding.

I think.

My second encounter with Cosell was much different. It took place in his office at ABC headquarters in New York City, in 1984. I had been sent by WTAE-TV, along with our new sports producer, Tim Kiely, and a cameraman to interview Howard about his decision to leave the "Monday Night Football" booth. It would be part of a Steelers pre-game show. Kiely, about 22 at the time, is the son of Ed Kiely, who spent most of his life working for the Steelers in media relations. Ed knew Cosell well enough that he was able to arrange for the interview.

If I hadn't had that earlier encounter with Cosell, I might have been nervous about doing a one-on-one interview with him, but I wasn't. We arrived at ABC headquarters early in the morning and were directed to a receptionist who had been expecting us. She pointed us in the direction of Cosell 's office and we all stepped inside and saw a guy who looked amazingly like Bela Legosi. (That's Dracula, for you youngsters out there).

He greeted us warmly by saying, "Who are you? What's this about? Who authorized this?"

Kiely, who was understandably intimidated and worried about a bad report getting back to his dad, started "Mister Coselling" Howard to death. "Hi, Mister Cosell, I'm Tim Kiely. I think you spoke to my dad, Ed."

Howard gave an impatient wave and said, "Yes, yes, I *re-mem-buh*. Let's get set up and get this over with."

I can honestly say that I wasn't the least bit bothered by the way Howard was treating us and not at all intimidated. It was exactly what I expected and, to be honest, kind of what I was hoping for.

Howard then went on to say, "WTAE Pittsburgh, John Conomikes (he was the station's general manager). You're not carrying my show." (Howard had a syndicated TV show at the time and was not happy that WTAE chose not to carry it.)

Howard wasn't finished.

"Myron Cope. He's a shill for the National Football League."

Then he gestured toward me and said, "You're a shill for the National *Foot*ball League." And he actually said it in that Cosellian way with an over emphasis on the word "foot." I said, "Howard, you don't even know me. How do you know that I'm a shill?"

"You're all shills for the National *Foot*ball League."

We ended up getting a good interview and when we wrapped it up he didn't rush us out of the office. He made small talk for a couple of minutes and made some off-the-record comments about his decision to leave "Monday Night Football." He was smoking a cigar and the sun was shining through the Venetian blinds and creating a pattern in the thick cloud of smoke around his head. I said something about him being bitter and he said, "*Bitt-uh*? I'm not *bitt uh*."

Then he said, "Do you want to talk about this on camera?" I, of course, said yes.

Howard is enveloped by an even larger cloud of cigar smoke and the sun is still shining through it making for an eerie special-effect when the tape rolls. I ask the question again and Howard does a great job of acting. He cocks his head as if it's the first time he's been asked the question and he says, "*Bitt-uh*? I'm not *bitt-uh*." Then he went on to explain why he wasn't bitter.

Guess what? He was bitter.

Another thing that sticks in my mind about that encounter was how Cosell spoke the same when he was making small talk with us as he did when the tape was rolling. When he was making an off-the-record reference to Commissioner Pete Rozelle he didn't say, "And I told Pete Rozelle" or "I told the commissioner." He actually said, "And I told Alvin Pete Rozelle...."

What a unique and entertaining man.

WHILE WE'RE ON THE SUBJECT

In case you were wondering what ever happened to the Kiely kid, he's done OK for himself. He's the Executive Producer of NBA basketball on TNT, which means he has almost daily dealings with a dominating and potentially intimidating personality named Charles Barkley.

I'm pretty sure he doesn't call him "Mr. Barkley."

CHAPTER 19

ONE, TWO, THREE, SHINK

I have no idea how many stories I did in my 30 years of working in local TV — it had to be somewhere around 2,000 — but I do know the one that got the most reaction.

It wasn't about Barry Bonds.

It wasn't about Kordell Stewart and it wasn't about any of the local teams.

It was about nothing.

That's what was happening on the fields where I used to play pickup games as a kid. I can't tell you what an advantage it was for me to be able to work in the town where I grew up and this was an example of a story that only someone who grew up in Western Pennsylvania could do.

I still live 15 minutes away from where I grew up in Scott Township. In 1983 I was living five minutes away from where I lived as kid and I noticed, when I passed the fields that I used to play on, that they were always empty. I wondered what kids were doing if they weren't playing baseball in the summer and football in the fall.

The fields got plenty of use at night, but that didn't count. Those were organized games with uniforms, umpires and snack moms.

I was wondering what happened to the pickup game.

I also saw an opportunity for an easy story.

So, I took a WTAE cameraman and went to the three or four fields where I used to play and to a few other neighborhood fields, stood in front of the camera and asked, "Where is everybody?"

I didn't provide any answers, just the question.

The first call I got was from Beano Cook. He complimented me on the piece and then went off. "What's wrong with these kids? What the hell do they do all day?"

The phone didn't stop ringing for an hour. All the calls were the same. Guys were asking what was wrong with kids and launching into stories about how they played pickup games every day.

At 7 o'clock I had to go downstairs to WTAE radio because I was filling in for Myron Cope. Every call was from someone who had seen my report and couldn't believe it. I came back upstairs to the TV newsroom and the phone was still ringing.

At 9 o'clock Stan Savran came upstairs from doing his talk show and said that his entire show was about the demise of the pickup game.

I continued to get reaction from people on the street for months.

I had obviously struck a nerve.

But here's the funny thing: When I bring this subject up around guys who are now in their mid-to-late thirties, they say, "Oh yeah. I can't believe these kids today. We played pickup games every day when I was a kid."

No, you didn't.

Not on the fields that I passed every day on my way to work.

I don't know when the pickup game disappeared but it was before today's middle-aged guys were kids. They may think that they played every day, but they didn't.

I did play pickup baseball every day in the summer, weather permitting.

It started with me and one other kid working the phones beginning around 9 in the morning. By 11 we knew what kind of a game we were going to have that day.

The perfect number was 12, six a side — three outfielders, two infielders and a pitcher. That meant right-field hitting.

We could make do with six, a pitcher, an infielder and an outfielder on each side. But that meant anything hit to the right of second base was an out.

It also meant we would play "pitcher's hand," which meant that the batter was out if he didn't reach first base before the pitcher either picked up the ball or caught the ball thrown by the infielder.

If we had two infielders, we played "pitcher's mound," which meant

104

that the batter had to reach first base before the pitcher had the ball, but the pitcher had to be on the mound when he received it.

The fact that somebody came up with "pitcher's hand" and "pitcher's mound" speaks volumes about the value of the pickup game. I have a feeling that neither was devised or suggested by an adult. I'll bet that the idea originated with kids who were looking for a way to make it possible to play baseball without nine on a side. Now nothing is done without adult supervision and the kids don't have to be creative and improvise because they only play in games that require uniforms, umpires and snack moms.

The two best players were captains and they "shinked it out" to see who got first pick. In other parts of the country they call it "shooting for it." One kid got "evens" and the other kid got "odds" and then, on the count of three, each kid threw out from one to five fingers. The winner was based on the combined number of fingers showing. In Pittsburgh, at least in my neighborhood, it was called "Shinking it out." Both players would say "One, two, three, shink" and then throw out their fingers. I apologize for having to explain all of this, but I have a feeling that there are lots of people who, sadly, are finding out about this for the first time.

There were kids who were always picked last and they dealt with it. Sometimes it was because of their age. Sometimes it was because they weren't quite as good as everybody else and sometimes it was because they stunk. A lot of the kids who were picked last got better over time and moved up in the ratings. Some never did. They all had to deal with it in their own way. It's called "life."

I interviewed a woman on my radio show in 2007 who had written a book in which she claimed that mothers needed to take more of an active role in their sons' athletic activities.

By the time the show was over, she didn't like me very much.

She couldn't understand why her suggestion that mothers need to be present on the rare occasions when boys are playing pickup games made me want to throw up all over the radio studio.

She bragged about how she liked to bring a lawn chair with her to the field while the kids were playing so that she could settle any disputes.

If she had brought a lounge chair to one of our pickup games, the only dispute would have been over who would get the honor of beating up her son.

When did kids become so dependent on their mommies?

This woman would have tried to tell us not to hurt anybody's feelings and pick teams based on the first letter of each player's name. You know, to be "fair." That would have lasted one day and we all would have quit and signed up for Boy Scouts.

Or soccer.

I interviewed another woman on the radio who took a lot of heat when she wrote a column in the New York Post about dropping her 9-year-old son off in Manhattan with subway tokens and a quarter to make a phone call and told him to get home on his own.

No problem.

Except for the people who wrote to the newspaper and called the New York City talk shows and demanded that the woman be charged with child abuse.

That woman liked me a lot when the show was over.

She now has a Web site that advocates less parental supervision.

When my son was about 12, the business manager of his hockey team (that's right, they have business managers) went around to all the parents and said that since there was some extra money in the treasury, he wanted to see if there was any interest in taking a trip. The team had played games in Columbus and Buffalo that year, so traveling was part of the deal.

Being the troublemaker that I am, I had a suggestion of my own. I said, instead of spending the money on motels and food, why not just buy some ice time for the kids, let them invite some friends and play a couple of hours of pickup hockey — something they had probably never done in their lives.

This guy, a very nice man who meant well, looked at me as though I had suggested that we dress the players in Shakespearean clothes for their next game. Actually, there was a much better chance of that happening because the mothers would have had fun making the costumes.

Needless to say, we took another trip.

See, giving the kids the ice time wouldn't have involved the parents and that was unacceptable.

That was 25 years ago and things have gotten much worse. The concept of kids organizing their own games has just about completely disappeared.

If you don't show up for every one of your kid's practices, you're a bad parent. If you don't show up for a game, there's a chance that you'll be getting a call from CYS.

My mother never saw me play a ballgame of any kind. My dad went to a few Little League games, but he usually showed up late because the games started before he got home from work.

I lived three or four miles from our Little League field and many times I put my uniform on, put my glove on the handlebars and rode my bike to the game. My bike wouldn't be the only bike parked at the field and on the way home there would be lots of other kids in their baseball uniforms riding on the same sidewalk.

I also remember piling into the car with several other players to go for ice cream after a lot of games. So, obviously, my parents weren't the only ones who weren't at the game.

Come to think of it, there were very few mothers at the games. I don't know how we survived without the snacks. I do remember one mother, who will remain nameless, who was notorious because she was so loud. She was also notorious just because she was the only mother who was at every game.

Today, nobody would notice her.

Back in the mid-'80s there was a controversy in Mt. Lebanon over the decision to build a soccer field in Bird Park, a small strip of woods in the middle of the township. The nature lovers wanted it left alone. The soccer parents wanted another field because too many 5-year-old girls were inconvenienced by the local soccer field shortage.

I lived about a mile from Bird Park and, because of my position as a local sportscaster, one of the local soccer moms approached me about throwing my support behind their group.

She wasn't happy when I told her that I thought that there were already too many fields and not enough woods. It could have been worse. I could have told her how much I hate soccer and consider it a game for socialists and communists. She tried to change my mind by telling me how inconvenient it was for her 7-year-old daughter, who had to get up early and/or travel a long way to soccer practice.

I had a feeling her 7 year old was only playing soccer because her mother told her that she wanted to. I based that on the fact that I had never seen a bunch of 7-year-old girls kicking a soccer ball around in somebody's back yard.

Here's a question for you: When was the last time you had to stop your car on a residential street to allow a kid to run out and retrieve a ball? I know it's been at least 25 years since I've had to do it.

The only way that's going to happen today is if one kid gets mad and throws another kid's video game out the window and on to the street.

Words can't describe how glad I am to have grown up when I did.

WHILE WE'RE ON THE SUBJECT

I'm a small-government guy with serious libertarian leanings. I want the federal government to have as little power as possible, mainly because I worry what would happen if someone like me became president and went berserk with power.

You know what I would do 15 minutes after I was inaugurated?

I'd issue an executive order to outlaw all fantasy sports.

Then, I'd set my sights on video games.

The whole idea of being a sports fan became distorted with the explosion of fantasy sports. Just watching the game used to be enough. Now, if an NFL telecast doesn't include the stats from every player in the league scrolling across the bottom of the screen, millions of fantasy nerds need medical attention. I guess it's fun for the people who do it, but I think the world would be a better place if people got back to just watching the game. At the very least, my world would be a lot less annoying.

Then there are video games.

There are millions of 20- and 30-something guys whose lives have either been ruined or are about to be ruined by an obsession with their joy stick. I'd like to see some stats on the number of softball leagues in operation now compared to 30 years ago. I'm way too lazy to look it up, but I'd be willing to bet there are nowhere near as many guys playing softball now as there were back then.

The thing that bothered me most about getting old — maybe the only thing that bothered me — was no longer being able to play ball. I played in competitive flag football leagues until I was 35 or 36. Most of the players on my team had played college football at some level, including Division

1. But they were out there on Sunday mornings, 10 or 12 years after their college careers had ended, still playing ball and taking it seriously.

And you're going to tell me that these guys sitting in front of a TV playing with a joy stick are having more fun?

Not a chance.

It's pathetic.

I can't imagine preferring a pretend version of football to playing the real thing.

I was still playing serious pickup touch football games when I was 35 and I was playing with the same guys I played with when I was 10.

When I was 30 and working for KQV and WDVE radio, I put together a team, "The Down, Out and Downers," that included guys from the two stations and some of my friends as ringers and I went on the radio and challenged all comers to games of six-man touch football. I rented a field in Lawrenceville and we played one game a week, under the lights, from September to December, and nobody ever beat us. I enjoyed those games more than any games I ever covered in any sport.

If you gave me the choice of going back in time to relive covering the Pittsburgh World Series, Super Bowl or Stanley Cup teams or re-playing that one season with the Down, Out and Downers, I'd take the DO&Ds and it wouldn't be close.

It's sad to think that millions of guys have traded that for playing Madden 2010.

You have to worry about the future of America when millions of adult men prefer spending time with something called "PlayStation" to actually spending time on a crisp fall night (or morning) diving in the end zone to catch a pass.

If I'm ever elected president, PlayStation is going to have to go, too.

Did I mention that words can't describe how glad I am to have grown up when I did?

WHILE WE'RE STILL ON THE SUBJECT

I'm sure that the Turkey Bowl is one of the last remnants of the pickup game, even among guys who stopped playing when the snack moms started showing up. Everybody has their stories of legendary yearly reunions of heated rivalries made up of opposing age groups or neighborhoods.

With us, it was the old guys against the youngsters.

I was one of the old guys, probably around 22 or 23, when the series started. The youngsters were still in college, between 19 and 21. Everybody who played was good and there were always several present or former college players in the mix. I think I was 40 when we played the last game of that series and I don't know who won the last one. I do know this: We never lost a game until Jack Ham and Mike Wagner showed up to play for us.

Yeah. That Jack Wagner and That Jack Ham.

I knew both of them pretty well but I wasn't responsible for recruiting them. One of the old guys was friends with both of them and had been badgering them to show up ever since they retired from the Steelers.

It's been a long time since the game so I don't have a lot of details. I just remember Ham dropping an interception that hit him right in the hands. To this day, when I see Wagner, I still blame the loss on him and his Hall of Fame buddy, but I can't remember what it was that he did to cost us the game. It's just something that both of them are going to have to carry with them for the rest of their lives.

By the way, Lynn Swann showed up to play for us the next year. He played quarterback and we won.

For some reason, he forgot to mention it during his Hall of Fame induction speech.

CHAPTER 20

SHORT STOP
A LOVELY FIRST DOWN

HERE'S something that would never happen in the 21st century:

The guys who played football behind Lincoln School at the corner of Beverly Road and Ralston Drive in Mt. Lebanon and who loafed on the corner there and hung out in the Beverly Road Isaly's, were known as "The Lincoln Bums."

It was an unofficial gang. No dues. No meetings. No official colors. No crack. No guns. Just teenagers loafing on the corner and playing pickup games in whatever sport was in season.

The Lincoln Bums were well known around Mt. Lebanon but not for anything other than being pretty good athletes who liked to have a good time. They had names like "Harpo," "Muz," "Huck," "Hoppy" and "Ferb."

Then there was "First Down."

Everybody just called her "First" and it's not for the reason you may be thinking. Patty Scarvis was her real name and she used to hang around as kind of the official unofficial female Lincoln Bum. She said very little and she was good looking. When she showed up at Isaly's, nobody ever said, "Hi, Patty." Hardly anybody knew her real name. It was, "Hi, First."

How did she get the name "First Down"?

Simple.

She used to hang around behind Lincoln School while the pickup games were going on and eventually was used as the official first-down marker. She was willing to move to whatever spot on the field where the team with the ball had to go for a first down and just stand there.

I don't know how many games it took before her name was changed, but I'm guessing it was only a few.

One more reason to love the lost art of the pickup game.

I wonder where "First Down" is now and if she ever told her kids and/ or her grand kids about this. I'll bet she never expected her name to show up in a book.

CHAPTER 21

'THE CHIEF'

WHAT did Art Rooney do to deserve the statue that stands outside Heinz Field?

You realize that he's the most inept team owner in North American history, right? Forget the fact that he managed to own a team that went 40 years without winning a championship. From 1933 to 1972 the Steelers had eight winning seasons. Break it down into decades and it's even more pathetic.

There were no winning seasons in the '30s.

Four in the '40s.

Two in the '50s.

And two in the '60s.

It wasn't until Art turned the operation of the team over to his oldest son, Dan, that the franchise advanced beyond laughing-stock status.

And that's why Art Rooney's statue is, or at least should be, the most inspiring of the four that stand outside the two sports facilities on the North Side. Everybody knows why Roberto Clemente, Willie Stargell and Bill Mazeroski will be there forever. They're not only three of the greatest Pirates of all time, they're three of the greatest baseball players ever.

"The Chief" got a statue because he was a nice guy.

How many people can say that?

I can't say that I knew Art Rooney well. I only knew him as well as someone from the media can get to know a team executive. I do know that

I knew him better than anybody who covered the great Dallas Cowboys teams of the '70s knew the Cowboys' owner Clint Murchison.

The Steelers opened the 1980 season with a Monday night game in Dallas and I was sent there a few days ahead of the game to produce some stories for a pre-game show on WTAE Channel 4.

I decided to do a piece comparing and contrasting the two franchises. I remember doing a standup in the parking lot of Texas Stadium and pointing out that it also doubled as a drive-in theater.

But what I remember most was talking to people in the Cowboys' office. I asked the receptionist sitting in the lobby how often Mr. Murchison comes into the office. She said, "I don't know. I've never seen him." I found out that he showed up there every couple of years.

The Steelers didn't have a receptionist in their office at Three Rivers Stadium. You walked into the lobby and waited until someone came out and asked if you needed help.

In September of 1977 I was about a month into my first job in the Pittsburgh media, working as Sports Director of KQV Radio. I had covered the team in training camp for less than two weeks and hadn't met "The Chief" or Chuck Noll and I was more than a little intimidated walking into that office for the first time.

I came through the front door, looked around for someone to help me and around the corner comes Art Rooney. I'm thinking, "Oh, boy. He's going to ask me for some kind of credential and I don't have one and he's going to either throw me out himself or call security. Or maybe call Jack Lambert."

Art Rooney walked up to me, a 29-year-old punk he had never seen before in his life, stuck out his hand and said, "Hi. What's your name?"

Not "Can I help you, sir?" Or "Excuse me, who are you with?"

Just "What's your name?"

I told him my name and who I was with and he didn't say, "What can I do for you?" Or "Do you have any ID?" Or "Do you have an appointment?"

He said, "Did your grandfather live on the North Side?" I told him that he did and Rooney said, "I think I knew him. Did they call him 'Lamp Post'?" I said I didn't know and for the next few minutes, the owner of the Steelers, who had never seen me before, and I made small talk.

I had a lot of conversations with "The Chief" over the years, almost never about the Steelers. He loved to talk about other sports and other teams. Especially the Pirates. He would show up a lot in the baseball press lounge at Three Rivers and offer his opinions on the game that night or the Pirates in general. And, just as important, he would ask *me* my opinion.

"The Chief" also liked hockey and he told me once that he would like to own the Penguins. He said he thought it would be easy to sell 15,000 tickets a game, which was then capacity at Mellon Arena.

A bankruptcy or two might have been avoided if he had followed through on that wish.

Rooney would also show up at Steelers practices at Three Rivers to talk to the media. Not in an official capacity. Just as an old guy who liked to shoot the shit. I remember a day when Chuck Noll was not in a good mood and told the media to stay in the home-plate area of the field, which was far removed from where the team practiced in the outfield.

"The Chief" walked up to a group of us sitting in the third-base dugout and said, "What are you guys doin' down here?" Somebody told him that Noll had told us to stay away and Art said, "What's he doin' out there, making an atomic bomb?" I think he thought that the football people took themselves a little too seriously.

Not long before he died in 1988, I was standing by myself on the field at Three Rivers waiting for the Steelers to come out for practice and "The Chief" sauntered up and said hello and we started making small talk.

I asked him if he was still taking his famous walks on the North Side every night. He said he was and I said, "Where do you go?"

He said, "I come down here," meaning Three Rivers Stadium. I asked him why he came down to the stadium and he answered, "To talk to the guys."

Now, this is the owner of an NFL team that had won four Super Bowls and when he says that he comes down to the stadium to talk to "the guys" I'm picturing him popping in on the coaches as they're looking at game films, so, I say, "You mean the coaches?" Art made a face and, in a tone dripping with impatience, said, "Noooo, the ground crew."

The Cowboys' receptionist hadn't seen *her* owner in a couple of years and this guy comes to the stadium every night to hang out with the ground crew.

I'll bet there aren't too many team owners who have taken their ground crew on the team charter and put them up at the team hotel. I traveled with the Steelers for many years and, until recently, there were always three or four ground-crew guys on every trip.

Art Rooney was a terrible team owner if you're judging him on wins and losses. I can remember as a kid hearing the old guys criticizing him for being cheap and being more interested in hiring his friends than winning.

As I said, I can't claim to have known him well. But I know enough about him to be pretty sure that he'd rather have a statue that honors him for being nice guy than for getting 3,000 hits, hitting 500 home runs or winning six Super Bowls.

CHAPTER 22

MY COUSIN CHUCK

CHUCK Noll gave me a very funny look the first time we met. It was September of 1977 and I had been working for KQV radio for about a month. I had covered the Steelers' training camp in Latrobe but we hadn't been formerly introduced and I had not done a one-on-one interview with him.

I spent almost 40 years sticking microphones in people's faces, but nobody ever intimidated me more than Noll. By 1977, Noll had already won two Super Bowls and had only missed his third in a row in 1976 because he lost his two starting running backs, Franco Harris and Rocky Bleier, before the AFC Championship game against the Raiders.

Back then, there was no live telecast of Noll's weekly press conference because there would have been no place to televise it unless a local station wanted to preempt a soap opera and, trust me, a president had to be assassinated for a station to risk incurring the wrath of the soap opera audience in 1977. (I was working at KDKA in 1986 when the newsroom phones were ringing off the hook with calls from old ladies who wanted to know when their "stories" were going to be back on. They had heard enough about the Space Shuttle Challenger blowing up.)

Believe it or not, Noll used to hold his press conference in the Three Rivers Stadium media lounge and it wasn't just for the media. There were lots of civilians there, too. The media consisted of a few beat writers from the local papers, three TV guys and a couple of radio guys like me. The press conference wasn't recorded, either. The writers took their notes and the radio/TV guys went outside to the baseball press box for one-on-one interviews after the press conference ended.

I took my tape recorder outside to the press box and waited my turn, which, because I was a new guy, came last. When you're the last guy in a group of one-on-ones with an important guy like Noll, you know that you're going to be asking him the same questions that he answered in the press conference and several more times in his interviews with the electronic media. That made me even more nervous.

Keep in mind that Noll had been hired to be the coach of the Steelers in January of 1969 when I was only 19 years old, so, for me, he still had that larger-than-life persona. He was 45 and already a coaching legend. I was about to turn 29 and about a month removed from being a door-to-door cable TV salesman.

Noll wandered over to where I was standing with my tape recorder and he had that "I've never seen you before, I'm about to be introduced" look on his face.

I stuck out my hand and said, "Hi, Chuck. John Steigerwald. I'm with KQV radio."

That's when I got the look.

I thought, "Oh boy, what snide remark could I have made about the Steelers that pissed him off? I've only been on the air for a few weeks."

Noll kind of pulled his head back and looked at me.

Then he said, "Are you from Pittsburgh?" I told him that I was and he said, "My mother's maiden name was Steigerwald."

Now, that was something that I was not prepared for.

It was also an excellent ice-breaker.

We talked about that for a few minutes and agreed that we could be long-lost cousins and I went ahead with the interview.

Noll only made two references to our "relationship" over the next 14 years. I do recall him calling me "Cuz" once, but I don't remember the circumstances.

He also made reference to it once in front of the whole world and I don't think anybody but I knew what he was talking about. It was at Super Bowl XIII in Miami. He was doing his first press conference in front of media from all over the world. Somebody asked him (for the thousandth time) if it bothered him that, despite his two Super Bowl wins, he wasn't mentioned in the same breath with guys like Don Shula and Vince Lombardi and the person also mentioned that Noll's name was often spelled wrong and that he was also often confused with another NFL head coach, Chuck Knox.

Noll brushed the question off and he nodded toward where I was sitting and said, "I guess I could use my other family name, like John's." That was it. Nobody in the room could have had any idea what he was talking about.

I liked it.

I don't think having the same name as his mother helped me at all when it came to dealing with Noll over the years. He gave me the same icy stare that he gave everybody else when I asked a question he didn't like, but I always respected Noll because he was a no-bullshit guy.

I don't think there is a phony bone in his body.

My favorite Chuck Noll comment came in response to a question posed to him by Pittsburgh Press columnist Phil Musick. Actually, it wasn't a question. It was a comment. By then, the press conferences had been moved to a conference room in the Steelers' office. Noll sat at the head of a long table and fielded questions from 10 or 12 reporters. There was still no live TV or radio coverage. It was a Monday in 1981, the day after a 38-10 win over the New York Jets. Noll didn't believe in pulling his starting quarterback when the Steelers got a big lead. He said he didn't like the message it sent to the rest of the team and he didn't think it was a good idea to make a backup come in cold off the bench.

So, Terry Bradshaw was still at quarterback for the Steelers when they had a 38-3 lead in the fourth quarter.

Musick said, "I talked to some of the Jets coaches and they said they thought you were rubbing their noses in it a little bit."

Noll got an impatient look on his face, and said, "I didn't see any white flags."

Perfect answer.

End of discussion.

BEST COACHING JOB EVER

The NFL's championship trophy might be named after the wrong guy. Calling it the "Vince Lombardi Trophy" back in 1970, shortly after Lombardi's death, made a lot of sense. Lombardi was already a legend and he was the winning coach in the first two Super Bowls, even though they were known then as the NFL-AFL Championship games.

Calling it the "Chuck Noll Trophy" might actually make more sense.

Noll is still the only guy to win four Super Bowls and he did a better coaching job with the Steelers in the 1970s than Lombardi did with the great Packers teams of the Sixties.

I'm here to tell you that from 1969 through 1979 Chuck Noll did the best coaching job in the history of North American professional sports.

Lombardi took over a pathetic Packers franchise in 1959 but he also inherited a roster that included Bart Starr, Paul Hornung, Forrest Gregg, Jim Ringo, Jim Taylor and Ray Nitschke, all of whom played major roles in his championships.

Don Shula won more games than any other NFL coach, but when he took over the Dolphins in 1970, he inherited Bob Griese, Larry Csonka, Jim Kiick, Larry Little, Mercury Morris, Nick Buoniconti, Manny Fernandez and Dick Anderson.

Those are all-pro-bowl players and many of them are in the Hall of Fame. It would be fair to say that Lombardi's and Shula's coaching had a lot to do with the players' individual success, but it would also be safe to assume, in Shula's case, that he was fully aware of the great young talent on the Dolphins roster when he agreed to leave the Baltimore Colts and take the job.

You can be pretty sure that Noll didn't take the job in Pittsburgh because he was convinced that the Steelers' roster was packed with future Hall of Famers. There were two players on the roster who could compare to the list of stars that Lombardi and Shula inherited — Andy Russell and Roy Jefferson.

Russell was a linebacker who has received some consideration from the Hall of Fame and Jefferson was one of the top five receivers in the NFL. Other than those two, Noll inherited Rocky Bleier, Ray Mansfield, a good offensive lineman named Bruce Van Dyke and a bunch of guys named Dick Arndt.

You would have to be at least 50 years old to understand what Noll got into when he took the job of Steelers head coach after Joe Paterno turned it down.

He had agreed to work in Football Hell or, at the very least, Football Siberia.

Pittsburgh was not a football town in 1969.

There are hundreds of thousands of people walking around Western Pennsylvania thinking that Pittsburgh was always the football capital of the world. They were all born after 1960.

Prior to 1972, the Steelers were something to do in between Pirates seasons and the Pitt football program in the late '60s was a disgrace to the university. How does 16-56 from 1966 through 1972 grab you? Pitt was so bad that in a 56-0 loss to Notre Dame at Pitt Stadium both teams agreed to keep the clock running in the second half. If they hadn't, Notre Dame would have scored over 100 points.

The Pirates were the Number One team in town. They had won a World Series in 1960 and had started every season since with a legitimate chance of winning a pennant.

When a comedian wanted to use a pathetic team in a comedy routine, he almost always used the Steelers. They had two winning seasons in the 1960s and a record of 45-72-6. That was after having two winning seasons in the '50s. Imagine the Steelers going from 2010 to 2029 and having only four winning seasons.

They were a lot better in the '40s, with three winning seasons.

We're talking about seven winning seasons in 29 years and, believe it or not, they were actually worse than their record indicated.

Football town, my ass.

The Steelers used to practice every day at the South Park Fairgrounds in those days and there wouldn't be 12 fans there trying to get a glimpse of them.

I remember paying a dollar for an end zone seat at Pitt Stadium and being surrounded by thousands of empty seats.

Noll was an assistant to Don Shula in Baltimore but that didn't impress anybody because Bill Austin was one of Vince Lomardi's assistants when he was hired by the Steelers in 1966.

He went 11-28-3.

Prior to Noll, the Steelers had two coaches who finished with a winning record. Jock Sutherland was 13-10-1 and Buddy Parker finished 51-47-6. That's two winning coaches in their entire history and combined the two of them were only seven games over .500.

You had to live with Steelers football for several years to really appreciate what Noll did. As impressive as it looks on paper for him to come within a fake punt by the undefeated Miami Dolphins of going to the Super Bowl just four years into his tenure, it's 10 times more impressive if you were there to see it.

At least it should be.

Turning a franchise around is one thing. It's been done many, many times, but no coach was asked to turn around a worse one than the 1969 Steelers because a worse one has never existed.

It would have been amazing if Noll had made the Steelers respectable. We all know what he did. He oversaw one of the greatest dynasties in sports history. If that wasn't enough, he did it with only players that he had drafted or signed as free agents. Not a single player on the 1978 and 1979 Super Bowl-winning rosters had ever played for another NFL team.

Noll's second decade wasn't nearly as good as his first, due in no small part to having to pick so late in the draft for so many years, and, by 1992, it was time for him to go.

Don Shula has the numbers and Vince Lombardi has the sainthood and they're widely considered the two best coaches in NFL history, but neither came close to doing the coaching job that Noll did from 1969 to 1984.

Nor has any other coach in any other professional sport.

Ever.

CHAPTER 23

NO MORE FRONT FOUR

FOR me, it wasn't about the principle. It was about the money. That's why I left Channel 4 (WTAE) in 1985. There was no other reason for me to leave. With Bill Hillgrove, Stan Savran, Myron Cope and me, we had the best and most popular TV sports department in town.

In seven years I had never had an argument or even a loud disagreement with any of the other members of the foursome. It was just that management at WTAE thought they could take advantage of me and I wasn't going to let it happen.

I beat them in the end and, as it turned out, they did me a huge favor. I ended up getting more money from KDKA for doing nothing than WTAE wanted to pay me for doing TV and radio and KDKA turned out to be, for all kinds of reasons, a much better place to work.

My experience will give you good insight into what goes on behind the scenes at your favorite TV station.

Every person you see on the air in Pittsburgh has a no-compete clause in their contract. It's kind of like the reserve clause, the mechanism that, before free agency, made it impossible for baseball players to have any say in where or for whom they played.

There is only one reason for any employer to insist on a no-compete clause—to avoid paying an employee what he or she is actually worth.

KDKA was willing to pay me to do nothing for a year rather than fight the no-compete clause because they had lots of their own people under contract who were bound by the same clause and had no interest in weakening it.

Don't feel too sorry for your favorite news anchor. He or she is well paid. Just keep in mind that there are still a few who could double their salaries if they were allowed to sell themselves to the highest bidder.

Left to right: Bill Hillgrove, me, Stan Savran and Myron Cope. The best TV sports team in Pittsburgh TV history, if I do say so myself.

My experience also gave me good insight into what negotiating is all about.

I learned that most of it is about bullshit.

I learned that nothing happens until there is a deadline. That's why, to this day, I pay very little attention to threats of a strike by players or a lockout by owners until the deadline is about to be reached. I never pay much attention to contract disputes between players and teams until the deadline arrives because I know that, in most cases, nothing will happen until then and everything that is said before it arrives is meaningless.

Most people don't work with a contract. Chances are that you work for a salary agreed upon when you were hired and you are free to leave your job for a better one at any time. TV people live their lives from contract to contract. Lots of them sweat it out wondering if they're going to be renewed. Management knows this. That's why they wait until two weeks before your five year contract is up before they start talking to you about a new one. It's in their best interest to make you sweat.

The reporter you see tonight may be a few days away from making it to the ninth month of his contract year and sweating whether he's going to make it past the deadline and be assured of having that next year picked up.

I had been working under a five year contract that I had signed a year and a half into the original five year deal that I had signed in 1978, so, in 1985, after seven years, I was getting my first real chance to negotiate. WTAE knew that I liked it there. They also knew that I was a Pittsburgh guy who had young kids in school and the last thing I wanted to do was move.

But, most importantly, they knew I had a no-compete clause that said I couldn't work for any other radio or TV station in the Pittsburgh market for a year.

I had kept my mouth shut for five years, even though I knew I was underpaid, because I assumed I would be taken care of on my next deal.

My attorney was a guy I had known since grade school. His name was Mike Burns and his dad and sister had done pretty well for themselves with contracts he negotiated for them with KDKA. He had told me several months earlier that KDKA's General Manager, Carolyn Wean, had told him several times that she liked my work. I asked Mike to call her and she immediately said she would be interested in hiring me, no-compete clause or not.

I was getting a good education in the art of negotiating. I didn't tell WTAE management that KDKA was interested. I enjoyed listening to them telling me how lucky I was to be getting the offer they were making and how lucky I was to be making so much money and how ridiculous I was being to expect more.

They were sure I wasn't going anywhere because of the no-compete clause. No one had ever beaten it before. I received an official offer from KDKA on a Friday, but, it was pending approval from Westinghouse headquarters in New York and my WTAE contract expired on Saturday. There was no guarantee that Westinghouse would go along with KDKA's plan to pay me to do nothing for a year.

I had a decision to make. I called the president of AFTRA, our union, and asked him how much severance pay I should expect to get. He said, "Why, have you been fired?" I told him that I hadn't but that my contract was expiring the next day. He said, "Then you call the boss and tell him you're not signing the contract but you're still a union employee and you'll be reporting to work on Monday." This forced WTAE into having to fire me to get rid of me and they didn't want to do that. They were still banking on that no-compete clause and figured I would come crawling back and I'm sure they had no interest in writing a severance check.

So, the following Monday I showed up for work at WTAE and was paid union scale, which wasn't much less than I had been making under contract. They told me I could no longer be a regular anchor and they said I would be only doing reporting and fill-in anchoring. I had to wait until the following Friday (the 13th, by the way) before finally getting the approval from Westinghouse. The plan was for me to sign a new deal on Tuesday with KDKA that not only was for more money than WTAE was offering but also included a country club membership and eight weeks paid vacation.

I went into WTAE on Monday for what I knew would be my last day, but I couldn't tell anybody. The Steelers were playing the Browns in Cleveland that night and both Bill Hillgrove and Stan Savran were covering the game, so I had to anchor the six and 11 o'clock newscasts. Little did anybody at Channel 4 know that the enemy was now among them. Believe me, it was a very strange experience sitting on that set, looking into that camera knowing that I was spending my last minutes at WTAE. You have no idea how badly I wanted to say, "And, by the way, I'm outta here. The next time you see me, I'll be working for the number one station in town, KDKA."

When the newscast ended I told everyone in the studio what had happened, said it was nice working with them and headed home feeling pretty good about myself.

I won.

The big, bad Hearst Corporation lost.

Hasta la vista, baby.

Everybody should experience the joy that I experienced the next day. I called WTAE news director Joe Rovitto and told him that I wouldn't be reporting to work. He said, "Why?" I said, "Because I just signed a five year, guaranteed contract with KDKA." Rovitto said, "John, you can't do that, you have a no-compete clause." I said, "They're going to pay me more to sit out and do nothing for a year than you guys wanted to pay me to do TV and radio."

There was a long pause on the other end of the line and then I heard this:

"Oh."

Rovitto was and still is a good friend of mine and I think he was just following orders when he offered me the embarrassing contract and it was obvious that he was disappointed.

Something else about TV contracts. Very few of them are guaranteed. Most of them are only guaranteed for one year. If you sign a five year deal it locks you into working for the station but the station can opt out each year by giving you 90 days notice.

Almost all the people you watch on TV have to sweat out the first nine months of their contract years wondering if the next year is going to be renewed.

WTAE had offered me a five-year deal with renewable options that would have allowed them to fire me after one year and still hold the no-compete clause over my head.

KDKA guaranteed all five years.

Then, all of a sudden, I was among the enemy. I was a Steeler who had been traded to the Browns. A Penguin who had been traded to the Flyers. And, make no mistake, KDKA was the enemy. That's who everybody else was shooting at. WTAE had gained a lot of ground in the ratings but there was no doubt among anybody working in the Pittsburgh market, who the giant was.

It was a very strange feeling walking into that enemy newsroom for the first time and I know it was strange for everybody there to see me in their newsroom.

I noticed the differences right away. KDKA had a full time public relations person. WTAE did not. KDKA was much more organized in the newsroom and took a much more thorough and professional approach to the day to day coverage of the news. I still felt quite a bit of loyalty to the on-air people I worked with at WTAE and I wasn't willing to concede that KDKA's "talent" (a term I despise) was any better. It would be a year before I would get a chance to work with them. I had no idea, when I was hired, what I would eventually be doing. No promises were made.

One thing I did know for sure was that our sports team at WTAE was better. KDKA had John Sanders, who graciously welcomed me and told me that I added credibility to their staff, which included Ken Mease, Alan Cutler, Steve Talbot, Bill Curry, still the best TV writer in Pittsburgh history, and a young producer/reporter named Bob Pompeani.

Mease, who eventually left and had a long career in Washington, D.C. and Talbot were pros. Cutler was a caricature of an airhead TV sports guy. Pompeani was a kid with a lot of talent who was just looking for opportunities to shine.

Two things struck me right away.

One, there was a lot of bickering. Most of it, it seemed to me, started by Cutler. There were arguments over who would get to do the live shot and whose package (report) would or should get more air time. In seven years at WTAE there was not one minute of that.

Two, they actually talked about the Pittsburgh Spirit as though they (it?) mattered. For you youngsters out there, the Spirit was (were?) Pittsburgh's team in the Major Indoor Soccer League.

These guys could actually identify more than two players on the team and, with the exception of Pompeani, who actually had the good sense to be a hockey fan, seemed to care more about the Spirit than they cared about the Penguins.

My brother, Paul, had the best description of what it was like to attend a Spirit game, something no serious sports reporter would do unless forced. He said it was like riding on a school bus. The Spirit couldn't sell tickets to regular human beings, so they packed the house with youth soccer teams.

I was the new kid, so I just kept my mouth shut.

Mease and Talbot left before I completed my year of exile, Cutler stayed on until after I was allowed on the air.

Sanders was as smooth as they come. Never made a mistake. He also was boring, but that's apparently what he and KDKA wanted, somebody who was safe, reliable and wouldn't offend anybody.

*A good blend of 1980's TV talent. Left to right, my brother Paul,
John Sanders, Bob Pompeani, me and the best writer for TV that
Pittsburgh has every seen, Bill Curry.*

In the days when local sports were actually considered vital to a TV news operation's success, it was important for a station to have a good "blend."

We had that at WTAE. Bill Hillgrove was the pro's pro who said all the right things, had a solid knowledge of sports, a good sense of humor and a good work ethic. Myron was Myron. Stan Savran was the super knowledgeable, hard hitting talk show host with strong opinions and the willingness to express them. I was something in between Stan and Myron. I wasn't shy about expressing my opinions and I took a more lighthearted approach with a good dose of sarcasm and cynicism mixed in.

At KDKA, Sanders, Mease and Talbot were about the same, Pompeani was young and enthusiastic and Cutler was unbelievably annoying.

KDKA News Director, Jim Hefner, had hired Cutler out of Lexington, Kentucky as his answer to Myron Cope. Cutler was from New York City, looked like Groucho Marx and covered sports with a New York City attitude. Only someone from outside the market would think that Cutler was a good fit for Pittsburgh. Hefner was from North Carolina and was determined to make Cutler a star, whether the ignorant people of Pittsburgh liked him or not.

A few months into my first year, some time early in 1986, Hefner called me into his office and asked me to close the door. He said, "I've made a big decision and I'd like to get your input. The decision has already been made but I know you grew up here, you have a background in baseball and you've worked in the market for several years. I'm putting Alan Cutler on the Pirates telecast. What do you think? Be honest and remember, the decision has already been made."

I said, "OK. You asked me. If you were to conduct a six month search to find the worst possible living person to add to the Pirates telecast, your search would end with Alan Cutler."

Hefner said, "OK. I respect your opinion, but I think you're wrong."

Cutler lasted about 15 minutes.

The producer and all the guys on the broadcast team wanted to strangle him by the bottom of the first inning of the first telecast.

That's how long it took before it was obvious that he was a terrible fit in the broadcast booth. After a few games they made him a roving reporter and had him interview fans. I'm pretty sure he was gone before the end of the season.

Hefner had accelerated Cutler's exit and before long he was back in Lexington.

About six months into my first year, Hefner called me into his office and showed me something that WTAE management would never consider showing their employees. He showed me my research. As in audience research. There was no better illustration of the differences between the two stations. WTAE wouldn't dream of sharing research with "talent" because "talent" might use it as ammunition during contract negotiations. Money was no object at KDKA. They paid huge money to their big time "talent" and everything they did was first class.

Hefner said, "Here. I want to show you why you're here." The research showed Myron Cope to be the most popular sportscaster in Pittsburgh by a ridiculously huge margin.

I was second.

That's when Hefner told me that, when I was allowed on the air in September, I would be anchoring the 11 o'clock sports.

It didn't take long for word to get to Sanders and it didn't take long for him to become a lot less friendly. We maintained a cordial, professional relationship but the long, deafening periods of silence coming from his adjacent cubicle made it pretty clear how he felt.

I have no patience for that, by the way.

If you're demoted or fired and I take your job, don't be pissed off at me. Be pissed off at the guy who demoted or fired you. Or be pissed off at yourself for not doing a better job.

Sanders was doing full time work in the Pirates broadcast booth and that meant that I would also be anchoring the six o'clock sports on many nights, which meant even less face time for him and more face time for me.

Not long after that, the new news director, Sue McInerney (Hefner had left to become General Manager at WTAE without having to sit out a year) came to me and said, "We're taking Sanders off the Steelers. I think they're going to stink this year and I want somebody who will say so."

I've never been paid a better compliment.

That was the beginning of my 20 years of being KDKA's "Steelers Guy" and doing "Steeler Monday" reports.

Within a year or so, Sanders was let go and I was installed as the six and 11 o'clock sports anchor.

In 1995, I was forced to take a 25 per cent pay cut, taken off the 11 o'clock sports and replaced by Bob Pompeani.

He and I haven't spoken off the air since.

I'm kidding.

The day that I got the news, I told Pompeani that I had no patience for people who resent the person who takes their job and I made it clear that I didn't resent him in any way. (I didn't.) I had big time resentment for KDKA's penny pinching General Manager, Gary Cozen, but I'd deal with that in my own way.

Cozen was slashing contracts all over the place and he would slash mine two or three more times. I developed a philosophy that helped me get through it and maybe it'll work for you if you're ever in a similar situation.

If they cut me 25 percent, I decided to care 25 percent less and, whenever possible, work only 25 percent as hard. When they cut me another 15 percent, that meant that I now cared only 60 percent as much as I used to.

I never felt guilty about continuing to take their money because I thought I had made a fair deal, even if I had only made it with myself.

I made a good living at KDKA and thoroughly enjoyed the first 10 years that I worked there. I tolerated most of the last 12 or 13 and was always hoping that they would fire me. They, of course, didn't want to fire me because they wouldn't have been able to enforce the no-compete clause and, while they didn't like paying me what they were paying me, they apparently preferred that to seeing me go to work for the competition.

All in all, I got into the local TV news business when the gettin' was good and I got out when the gettin' was even better.

CHAPTER 24

SHORT STOP
RADIO DOG

ONE of the best gigs I ever had was "working" on the WDVE Morning Show with Scott Paulsen and Jimmy Krenn. The station installed a microphone in my basement game room and, twice a week, I would sit in front of it, in my underwear, and field — let's call them "non-traditional" — questions from the boys.

A hundred bucks a pop for five minutes of laughing and scratching.

During one of my appearances, I decided to introduce one of my three dogs, Melvin. He was a typically goofy English Springer Spaniel who never left my side. So, when I was doing the radio, he was sitting there right next to me.

Melvin had a girlfriend named Sheba whom he had been separated from a year or two earlier when we moved. I could get him to howl by simply saying, "Melvin, where's *Sheeeeeba*?"

Sometimes I wouldn't even have to stretch out the name. I could matter-of-factly say, "Uh, Mel, I wonder where Sheeba is?" and he would start. It wasn't just your basic spaniel howl. We're talking about a long, drawn-out howl that sounded like an air-raid siren. He'd throw his head back, pucker his lips and blow it out on cue.

Perfect for the radio.

So, one day, I told Scott and Jim about Mel and how much he missed his girlfriend. I laid a "*Sheeeba*" on him and he went off. I held the microphone in front of his mouth for at least 20 seconds and let him rip. Mel became a regular on the show.

A few months later my wife Jeani and I were out walking Melvin and our other dog, Irving. Two women were walking in the opposite direction across the street and as they passed, I heard one say, "Hey, there's that dog who's on the radio."

I'm not sure, but I think I saw Mel give Irv a little nudge.

CHAPTER 25

HITCHIN' A RIDE

I made one of the smartest moves in my career in 1998.

I had just seen a report that CBS, which had been without NFL football for several years, had won the rights to televise AFC games. That meant the Steelers' games would be on KDKA. It was after 11 o'clock at night, but I called the General Manager, Gary Cozen, at home because I knew he would be shocked and excited.

Sometime during that conversation I suggested that any deal he negotiated with the Steelers for preseason games should include three seats for KDKA people on the team charter for the entire season. Cozen, because of his almost psychopathic cheapness, had been torturing KDKA employees for a few years with ridiculous and sometimes inhumane travel arrangements. He established a policy of only traveling on trade, which meant that cash would not be used to buy airline tickets. The station would get plane tickets in exchange for airtime. That was a nice deal for Cozen's bottom line and his insane need to feel like he squeezed every last dime out of whomever he was doing business with, but it was tough on reporters who were traveling on assignment. The airlines only made certain flights available for trade and that made for some creative travel arrangements.

Cozen did a great job of taking every ounce of enjoyment out of every assignment. For example, instead of hopping on a plane in Pittsburgh and flying directly to Sarasota/Bradenton Airport for Pirates spring training in Bradenton, your trip would be cozenized to include an early morning flight to Newark, a four-hour layover, a flight to Tampa and a one-hour drive to Bradenton. Hotels were done on trade, too, and let's just say there weren't any five stars that were willing to trade rooms for airtime.

I wouldn't expect anybody to feel sorry for someone who's being paid to go to spring training for a week, but Cozen succeeded in taking every bit of glamour and pleasure out of that assignment.

Our Steelers trips had become pretty annoying, too. Lots of long layovers in out-of-the-way airports and nights spent in dumps. I had to switch out of a hotel in Washington, D.C., after I saw three roaches run across the floor.

Keep in mind this was KDKA, where everything used to be first class. One more example of how the enjoyment can be taken out of the best assignments:

In January of 1998, during the week leading up to the AFC Championship Game in Pittsburgh, I was called into the operations manager's office. She was unfortunate enough to be in charge of helping Gary Cozen trip over dollars to get to pennies. The news director and a few other managers were there. They had something really funny to tell me. The Super Bowl travel plans to San Diego had been cozenized. This, of course, was dependent upon the Steelers beating the Broncos in a few days. For the Super Bowl trip to San Diego, the majority of the KDKA travel party would fly from Pittsburgh to LAX in Los Angeles and then drive to San Diego the Monday before the game. After the game, the people who had worked all day unpacking, packing and hauling equipment around, would drive (in post Super Bowl traffic) to LAX — probably a 1½-hour trip.

Then they would hop on the redeye at midnight.

But they wouldn't be flying to Pittsburgh. They would fly right over the tops of their homes and go to Philadelphia and land at 5 a.m. before catching a 10 o'clock flight to Pittsburgh.

Have you ever taken the redeye from the West Coast?

If you have, you know that, when you get off the plane, you feel like one large ball of grease. How about making someone work all day, drive an hour and a half to the airport for a 6-hour flight, followed by a 5-hour layover, followed by another 45-minute flight?

The management types thought that I would laugh when they told me of Cozen's latest diabolical plan, but this time I didn't. I told them that there aren't many people who are better than I am at finding humor in just about any situation, but there was nothing funny about what they had just told me and that Cozen should be tossed out into the street and never allowed back in the building.

So, while you were watching KDKA-TV's coverage of the excitement leading up to that 1997 AFC Championship game, with the anchor women wearing their mandatory black and gold — Yep, it's *mandatory*; I know of anchor women who were sent home if they weren't wearing the team colors — little did you know that many of the people you were watching were hoping the Steelers would lose, including KDKA management, led by Cozen, who was probably suicidal from looking at what it would cost the station. And, while you may think that they were spoiled and that you would have jumped at the opportunity to follow that itinerary for a free trip to the Super Bowl, you're wrong.

It's different when you're a fan. Very few of the KDKA people who would have made the trip to the Super Bowl would have seen the game in person. They would have been stuck in a press tent somewhere watching it on a TV from across the room.

Trust me.

It ain't as glamorous as you think.

When Gary Cozen was involved, every trip was a trip to and from Hell.

Traveling on the Steelers charter is the exact opposite of what I just described. There is no better way to travel unless you have your own plane.

Allow me to break down a typical Steelers trip:

Leave home about 1 p.m. on Saturday and head to the FBO hangar at the airport. That's where the Steelers' plane was parked.

Park my car in an indoor lot that is about 150 yards from the door of the plane.

Go through a security check in the hangar. (More on that in a minute.)

Grab a plastic bag and pick from a smorgasbord of food that included sandwiches, shrimp cocktail, chips, pretzels, cookies and candy bars and drinks (non-alcoholic).

Walk a couple of hundred feet to the plane and walk up the stairs and in the back door (the coaches and players use the front door and sit in the front of the plane) to my reserved seat a few rows from the back of the plane. On most trips the middle seat was empty.

Within a few minutes of the 2 o'clock takeoff, despite the fact that we all were able to load up on food before we got on the plane, the flight attendant comes around to ask me for my meal choice.

After the meal, the flight attendants come down the aisle offering Dove ice cream bars and other desserts. (There were a few members of the regular traveling party who never turned down anything, no matter how much they had already eaten and they looked it.)

The plane lands and we de-plane from the back door right on to the tarmac and walk about a 100 feet to the media bus.

The four or five buses would then head for the hotel with a full police escort. (I always thought this was a little excessive since we were usually arriving mid-to-late Saturday afternoon and there was rarely any traffic to speak of.)

Upon arrival at the hotel, we de-bus and enter the hotel through a special entrance. The players do their best job of acting like they're not annoyed by the screaming Steelers fans who are cordoned off by police tape.

Inside the hotel, there's no checking in. My key is sitting on a table in an envelope with my name on it.

Hop on the specially reserved elevator and go to my room.

The return trip was even easier.

After the game, get on the bus, get off the bus on the tarmac, board the plane, where I would find a bag full of snacks and maybe a nasty looking sandwich or two on my seat; wait for the flight attendant to ask which meal I prefer, decide whether I'm interested in the desserts that are constantly moving up and down the aisle, de-plane in Pittsburgh, walk a few hundred feet to my car and drive home.

Can you see why a person could be spoiled by that?

Do you see why it was important for me to get seats on the plane as part of any TV deal? It was a veteran move on my part that is still paying off for the boys at KDKA.

Of course I appreciated those seats even more after 9/11/2001, when flying commercial became much more of a nightmare.

The Steelers charter was affected by the heightened security and it's a perfect example of the overkill that takes place in airports every day.

Since 2001, when you arrive at the FBO for the Steelers' charter, you are met by airport security people who check your bag and make you take off your shoes.

I think most fans would get a kick out of seeing Bill Cowher (now Mike Tomlin, of course) and Dan Rooney being asked to take off their shoes. Do you feel safer knowing that the federal government is doing everything it can to protect you from Dan Rooney suddenly becoming a shoe bomber and blowing the team plane out of the sky above the Parkway West?

I know I do.

WHILE WE'RE ON THE SUBJECT

As I write this, Osama Bin Laden is apparently still at large. I bring this up here because I just spent the last 1,500 words or so talking about travel and how I was spoiled for life by traveling with the Steelers. I would be OK if I never set foot in another airport and it's all because of what happened on 9/11/2001. We need to make this guy pay for the death of almost 3,000 people and, there are lots of opinions on how that should be done.

He could die by lethal injection and that would make lots of people happy.

Or he could do life imprisonment in a 9x7 cell.

The death penalty is too easy and is exactly what he would want because he could achieve martyrdom. I would prefer life in a 9x7 with no Koran, no magazines, no radio and no TV, but even that would be letting him off too easy.

Here's what I would do: (It's also another example of why I should never be put in charge.)

I would capture him alive and bring him back to New York and I would build a hut for him adjacent to the busiest security gate at La Guardia Airport. The hut would be big enough for a cot, a toilet, a shower and not much else.

Then, I would give him a nice shave and fit him for a three-piece suit and get him a nice tie and a pair of dress shoes with laces.

Definitely with laces. Lots of them.

Maybe a nice hanky for his pocket and a really nice shirt with cuff links and a really nice belt with a big, shiny buckle. Make him look and feel like a successful American businessman.

He would sleep in the hut and be awakened every morning at 5:30 and be made to put on his nice, new clothes.

Put a nice, bulky piece of carry-on luggage and a big, heavy topcoat in his hands and take him to the back of the longest line at security and, when he gets to the end, make him take of his shoes, put them and his topcoat and his bag on the belt and walk through the metal detector. Remind him to take off his cufflinks and tell him to remove his belt.

Thank him for his cooperation and tell him to go to the back of the line and do it again.

All day.

From six in the morning until eight at night.

Seven days a week.

Fifty-two weeks a year.

If he starts to balk at putting the clothes on, encourage him with a cattle prod.

Travelers would be encouraged to laugh at him and ask him if he's enjoying his stay in New York.

When he gets back to the hut at 8 o'clock, he can watch TV. But the only thing on the TV will be a continuous five-minute loop of the planes hitting the World Trade Center. He loved those pictures when he saw them live.

A week of that and he'd be begging to be hanged.

Make it a life sentence and hope that he lives to be a hundred.

CHAPTER 26

SHORT STOP
HEY, JOE

I'VE never met Joe Namath but my college roommate, Paul Nolan, did and I always liked this story. "Mooner," as he was known, because former major league outfielder Wally Moon was his favorite player when he was a kid, went to the notorious Bachelors III club in Fort Lauderdale in the winter of 1969. It was notorious because Namath was part owner and there were rumors that it was also owned by a bunch of guys named Vinnie and Sal who used to like to book a bet every now and then. The NFL told Namath he had to sell his share and it became the biggest sports story in the country for a while.

Keep in mind that, at the time, if Namath and Paul McCartney had walked into a room together, Namath would have drawn the biggest crowd and ended up with the nicest chicks.

He was a mega-star.

Mooner was a 22-year-old kid from McKees Rocks (actually Kennedy Township, but those guys always said they were from "The Rocks"), who had flunked out of Kent State and was fooling around before going back to school.

Namath comes walking by and, while everybody else is in awe and just stares, Mooner sticks out his hand, palm up and says, "Joe, McKees Rocks."

Namath, without breaking stride, smiles, says, "Beaver Falls" and slaps him five.

I always thought that was very cool and I thought it said a lot about Namath knowing where he came from. Most guys would have either given Mooner a quick "Nice to see ya" or ignored him.

Namath knew that Mooner knew he was from Beaver Falls but he knew that "Beaver Falls" was the perfect response to "McKees Rocks."

Again, very cool.

At least I thought so.

CHAPTER 27

KORDELL

I T was a Tuesday, several weeks into the Steelers' 1998 season. Bill Cowher was presiding over one of his extremely annoying snooze conferences and the subject was Kordell Stewart and the Steelers' offense, neither of which was doing very well.

I began what was going to be a question by saying, "You guys don't use a lot of play-action…." Cowher interrupted me, saying, "Wait a minute. I'm not going to agree with your premise. We had a lot of play-action plays on Sunday." I said, "I counted three."

To which Cowher replied, "You counted wrong."

Talk about compelling live television.

That was the end of my question. The previous week I had read a column in the Sporting News about Stewart. The writer was listing the many reasons for Stewart not being able to play as well as he had played when he took the NFL by storm in 1997.

He had watched tapes of several Steelers games and counted a total of only six play-action passes by Stewart. That's why I decided to count them in the next game and I counted three.

Not long after the press conference ended, I was in the media lunchroom at Three Rivers Stadium eating my free meal and shooting the shit with my media buddies.

Ron Wahl, the Steelers' media relations director, came to our table, tapped me on the shoulder and said, "Coach would like to see you in his office."

I said "OK," although I did find it a little strange. On the way to the office, Wahl told me that "Coach" wanted to discuss the play-action issue with me.

I walked into Cowher's office and found him sitting behind his desk. I remember thinking what little chance there would ever have been of Chuck Noll inviting a media shlub into his office to clarify one of his answers. I sat down and Cowher immediately started going over the play-by-play sheet from the previous game.

He counted six play-action passes by Stewart, but he included three shovel passes, which I never considered play-action. It was a friendly conversation and, on the way out the door, I said, "I never considered a shovel pass a play-action pass." Cowher said, "Actually, neither did I. I just kind of threw them in there."

So, my premise had been correct. Stewart had only thrown three passes that had been preceded by a fake.

This was no small point. Stewart was stinking up the league and was on his way to eventually being made into a wide receiver by Cowher. The fact that a guy who, at that time, was the best running quarterback in NFL history and who played for a team that was more committed to running the ball than any pro team since the invention of the forward pass, was not taking advantage of that by using play fakes was ridiculous.

Bill Cowher was well on his way to ruining Kordell Stewart's career.

By then, most of the fans had turned on Stewart and most of the media had, too.

I was on my way to risking my career by standing up for Stewart.

Before it was over I would be called "a nigger lover" and a "faggot." My friends in the media would tell me to get over it and so would members of my immediate family.

I knew I was right and everybody else was wrong.

I had never said that I thought Stewart was on his way to the Hall of Fame or even the Pro Bowl. I simply disagreed when just about everybody in the Steeler Nation was saying the Steelers couldn't win with Kordell Stewart at quarterback.

I saw him play in 1997, when the Steelers went 12-6 and lost to the eventual Super Bowl winner in the AFC Championship game.

I saw him outplay John Elway on a Monday night at Three Rivers

Stadium, when he had 300 yards passing, threw three touchdown passes and ran for two touchdowns.

I saw him outplay Brett Favre on a Monday night at Three Rivers Stadium in 1998 when he put up a 117 passer rating.

I heard his teammates say that he was a future superstar.

I heard Jim Sweeney, an offensive tackle from Pitt, compare him to Dan Marino. I saw him become the only quarterback in NFL history to run for more than 10 touchdowns and throw more than 20 touchdown passes in the same season. (As I write this, he's still the only one to do it.) I saw him make the longest TD run by a quarterback in NFL history.

I also saw him lose his offensive coordinator, Chan Gailey after the 1997 season.

I saw him lose his best receiver, Yancey Thigpen, after the 1997 season. (At this writing, Thigpen's 1,398 yards receiving that season are still the most in Steelers history.)

I saw him lose his starting left tackle, Pro-Bowler John Jackson, after the 1997 season.

I heard people in the Steelers organization say that the offensive coordinator who replaced Gailey, Ray Sherman, "Didn't have a clue" and had to ask other assistants for help in identifying plays.

I saw him stink in 1999 and be not only benched, but turned into a wide receiver and told that he could no longer attend quarterback meetings. But I had also noticed that he had lost his best receiver again after the 1998 season when Charles Johnson left as a free agent. He also lost his Hall of Fame-caliber center, Dermontti Dawson and his starting right tackle, Justin Strzelczyk for nine games each — and this was after his all-pro left guard Wil Wolford had retired after the 1998 season.

In 1999 he was playing for his third offensive coordinator in three years, Kevin Gilbride, who told him he ran too much and was known to yell at him after 30-yard runs.

His top three wide receivers to start the '99 season had combined for one touchdown catch the previous season. His go-to guy would be Courtney Hawkins, a 5'9" journeyman at the end of his career.

One of those three receivers was a kid named Hines Ward, who had to beg Gilbride, the offensive genius, for playing time.

Through all of this, the Steelers were losing and the fans were booing and making up stories about Stewart's sexual orientation.

(By the way, the fans who spread those rumors needed to see the woman who used to wait for Stewart outside the Steelers' locker room. She looked like Halle Berry.)

Mark Madden, who had the most influential talk show in town at the time, was relentless. He referred to Stewart as the worst quarterback in NFL history.

Meanwhile, I was defending him in newspaper columns and on the "Sunday Night Sports Showdown" on KDKA-TV and getting angry phone calls and e-mails from fans wanting to know why I didn't just give it up.

Things turned in the 2000 season.

Cowher and Gilbride showed how clueless they were by going out and signing Kent Graham to play quarterback. He made up for having a less-than-mediocre career with the Giants by having the biggest ass ever on an NFL quarterback.

I never checked his shoe size but I'm guessing 16 EEE.

There may never have been a quarterback more unable to get out of his own way than Kent Graham.

Instead of putting "GRAHAM" on the back of his jersey, they should have put "NOT STEWART."

He was the perfect anti-Kordell.

Gilbride wouldn't have to worry about yelling at this guy after 30-yard runs.

Stewart was moved back to quarterback after being humiliated by Cowher in 1999, but he started the regular season as Graham's backup.

Graham played so well in his first game as a Steeler that they were shutout by the Ravens, 16-0.

In the second game of the season, Graham made one of the worst plays in Steelers history when he managed to get sacked near the Browns' goal line and allow the clock to run out before the Steelers could line up for a field goal in a 23-20 loss.

Stewart had never looked so pathetic.

But Graham was still the man for Game 3. If there were any plans afoot to turn him into a tight end, the coaches did a good job of keeping it quiet.

The Steelers were 0-3 after a loss at home to the Titans and, after going 7-9 in 1998 and 6-10 in 1999, Bill Cowher, who had survived a power struggle with Director of Football Operations Tom Donahoe, when Donahoe was fired after the '99 season, was well on his way to his third disastrous season in a row.

And he deserved every bit of it.

Guess who saved him.

Yep, the guy he had humiliated the year before. Graham was hurt in the loss to the Titans and Stewart got the start in Game 4 at Jacksonville.

The Steelers won the game. Stewart wasn't spectacular. He was barely passable, but he didn't do any damage, ran for 61 yards and played at least as well as Graham had played the first three games.

Stewart, only because Graham was still hurt, got the start against the Jets the next week and was 17 for 26 for 140 yards and one touchdown with no interceptions. The Steelers won again. His critics grudgingly admitted that he played pretty well.

Of course, when the Steelers played the Bengals at Three Rivers Stadium the next week, Graham got the start and Kordell rode the pine. Not because of what Graham had done in the first three games or what Stewart had done in the next two.

Because of what Stewart had done in 1998 and 1999.

It wouldn't be the last time he had to pay a big price for those two seasons. It wasn't long before Graham's large ass got him knocked out of commission again and Cowher and Gilbride had no choice but to stick with Stewart as the starting quarterback.

His record as a starter was 7-4, compared to Graham's 2-3.

Without Stewart, Cowher would have been looking at another 7-9, 6-10 or worse season and Dan Rooney would have spent the next several months trying to justify keeping Cowher and letting Donahoe go.

Most of the fans and the talk show hosts continued to give Kordell as little credit as possible and point to the fact that he was only averaging about 25 passes a game and rarely threw for more than 200 yards. (I noticed in 2004, when a rookie named Ben Roethlisberger went undefeated by throwing even less, that was almost never brought up.)

I wasn't ready to say "I told you so" yet, but I wouldn't have to wait long.

Stewart went to training camp in 2001 as the Steelers starting quarterback. He would have to adjust to another new offensive coordinator, but, for the first time since Chan Gailey left after the 1997 season, he would be playing for a guy who didn't try to turn him into Kent Graham.

Mike Mularkey had a clue.

He understood that the most dangerous running quarterback in NFL history should not only be allowed to run, but that he should take advantage of the threat to run by using a lot of bootlegs, play-action passes and play-action runs.

Stewart and the Steelers started that season with a 21-3 loss in Jacksonville. Stewart went 21-37 for 181 yards with one interception and a 47.2 passer rating.

Amazingly, Cowher didn't turn him into a wide receiver again.

He wasn't much better the next week in Buffalo, going 15-22 for 107 yards in a 20-3 win.

The Steelers started winning games by running the ball, winning the time of possession battle and playing tremendous defense. Stewart wasn't hurting them and, at the time, that was considered a major accomplishment.

But Stewart would soon start to make his case for being the team MVP.

From Game 4 through Game 15, the Steelers, playing with the quarterback they could never win with, went 10-2. During that stretch, Stewart completed 61 percent of his passes with 14 touchdown passes and seven interceptions. But four of those interceptions came in Game 15, a 23-20 overtime loss to the Bengals. Jon Kitna threw 68 passes in that game, completing 35 of them for 411 yards.

During that 12-game stretch, Stewart — the stupid, inaccurate passer who couldn't read defenses — had nine games in which he threw no interceptions. He actually had a stretch of 13 games when he threw a total of three interceptions. I defy you to find a starting quarterback in Steelers history who had fewer than 3 interceptions in any 13-game stretch. He also ran for 442 yards to go with his 2,597 yards passing. The Steelers, who couldn't win with this guy at quarterback, averaged 26 points a game during that 12-game stretch and finished 13-3.

CBS analyst and former Giants quarterback Phil Simms was a guest on my radio show near the end of the 2001 season and he told me that he wasn't surprised by Stewart's success because he had good receivers, a good running game and an offensive coordinator who knew how to use him. He also told me that, in 1999, when the Steelers hired Kevin Gilbride to be their offensive coordinator, he remembered thinking that the Steelers couldn't have found a worse match for Stewart if they had tried. He also said, "I never expected him to have success in that system."

Stewart's teammates voted him their Most Valuable Player and he finished third in the voting by opposing players for league MVP. He received more votes than any other player in the AFC.

I wrote my "I Told You So" column in the Pittsburgh Tribune-Review right around Week 14.

I was right and just about everybody else was wrong. (I do remember that Ed Bouchette, who's been covering the Steelers for the Post-Gazette for more than 25 years, agreed with me and continues to believe that Stewart got a bad deal.)

The Steelers could win with Kordell Stewart at quarterback if he was allowed to be Kordell Stewart.

Then Stewart went out and lost the AFC Championship game to the Patriots. Ask any Steelers fan today why the Steelers didn't beat the Patriots and go to the Super Bowl in 2001 and he'll say, "Kordell Stewart."

This despite the fact that the Steelers gave up two special-teams touchdowns and lost by seven points. The Patriots returned a punt for a touchdown and got another on a return of a blocked field goal. Jerome Bettis, who had missed the last five games of the regular season with a groin injury, made it obvious that he came back to soon (another terrible coaching decision by Bill Cowher) and finished with eight yards on nine carries. Through no fault of Stewart's, the Steelers fell behind 21-3 and were taken out of their ball-control game.

It was a team loss but Stewart took most of the blame because of his three interceptions and because of those two bad seasons in 1998 and 1999 and just because.

That loss would also play a part in Stewart being benched again in

2002 when Cowher put the final touches on the ruination of Stewart's career.

The Steelers opened the 2002 season on the road against the defending Super Bowl Champions. The Patriots were also playing their first game in brand new Gillette Stadium. Kordell "lost" this game, too. Yep, even though Tom Brady completed 29 of 43 passes for 294 yards and three touchdowns and despite the fact that it was 10-7 at half time and one of the Patriots' TDs was set up by Jerome Bettis' first fumble in 760 carries, this was one more loss blamed on Stewart.

He threw a couple of ugly interceptions early in the game but had taken the Steelers on a long drive that could have resulted in the tying touchdown. But Plaxico Burress stupidly stepping on the boundary at the back of the end zone after Stewart had scrambled and made a perfect pass on the run — followed by a stupid unnecessary roughness call on the one yard line that put the ball back at the 16 and a missed field goal — meant the Steelers came away with nothing and never got close again.

But it was all Kordell's fault.

The Oakland Raiders came to town for Game 2, which meant that the Steelers opened their season against the defending Super Bowl Champions and the team that would represent the AFC in the next Super Bowl. Rich Gannon threw for 403 yards in this one and the Steelers lost. Of course, this one was also Kordell's fault. He actually outplayed Rich Gannon in the game and finished with a higher passer rating but he fumbled a snap near the Raiders' goal line and everybody in Pittsburgh was programmed to believe that it had to be Stewart's fault and couldn't possibly have anything to do with the center.

Gannon had two passes intercepted inside the Steelers' five yard line but they were attributed to great plays by the Steelers defense, not a stupid quarterback who couldn't throw accurately or read a defense.

When the Steelers fell behind the Browns the next week at Heinz Field and Stewart was intercepted in the end zone, Bill Cowher decided to bench the guy who had saved the season for him a year earlier for a guy who hadn't started an NFL game in five years and had been selling insurance for four years before playing one season in the XFL.

The "Kordell Stewart Era" was over and the "Tommy Gun Era" had begun.

Think about what Cowher had done to Stewart. He benched his 2001 MVP two-and-a-half games into the 2002 season. The '98 and '99 seasons were rearing their ugly heads again. There is no way Cowher, without the memory of those two disastrous seasons, would have given up on his starting quarterback and MVP so early.

Stewart had not played well in his first three games but lots of quarterbacks go through stretches when they struggle.

That same year, Brett Favre had a combined three touchdown passes, seven interceptions and a 40-something passer rating in back-to-back games. Peyton Manning had a combined three touchdown passes and five interceptions in back-to-back games.

In games three and four that year, Steve McNair had three touchdown passes and seven interceptions. He wasn't turned into a wide receiver. The previous season, Drew Bledsoe had a stretch of three games when he threw two touchdown passes, six interceptions and put up passer ratings of 61.6, 43.4 and 41.3. And none of those numbers came in back-to-back games against teams that were months removed from the Super Bowl.

All of those quarterbacks kept their jobs and none was turned into a wide receiver.

Of course none of those quarterbacks had seasons as bad as the ones Stewart had in '98 and '99.

Cowher panicked.

For a while it looked like a good move.

Tommy Maddox was everything Stewart was not. He was decisive, he exuded confidence and he was white.

That's right. He was white. He played white. Which meant that he didn't scramble around. He stayed in the pocket and got rid of the ball. And, since he was white, he was obviously less dependent on his athletic ability and got by on his intelligence and ability to read defenses.

The fans were ready for a new savior and the media were ready for a new story. Maddox was "The Comeback Kid."

He also was the worst thing that ever happened to Bill Cowher.

The Steelers went 10-6 and made the playoffs, but, during that time, Maddox played some of the worst games ever played by a Steelers quarterback. When he was good he was very good and when he was bad he was really, really bad.

But, no matter how bad he was, he wasn't bad enough for the Steelers' reigning MVP to get his job back. In games one, two and three, Stewart was 64 for 118 for 728 yards, two touchdowns and six interceptions. Maddox, in games 10, 13 and 14 was 57 for 96 for three touchdowns and five interceptions. Stewart, because Maddox was hurt, started games 11 and 12 and played flawlessly and the Steelers won them both. But the reigning MVP took a seat on the bench when Maddox came back for Game 13.

That's when Maddox played what may have been the worst game ever played by a Steelers quarterback and the Steelers lost 24-6 to the Houston Texans, an expansion team. Maddox had two interceptions and a fumble returned for touchdowns. The reigning team MVP stayed on the bench for the rest of the season including a playoff win over Cleveland in which Maddox played, by far, the worst first half ever played by a Steelers quarterback in a post-season game. Only a dropped pass on third down by Dennis Northcutt with a little over two minutes to go in the game made it possible for Maddox to pull one out of his keyster. Stewart never played another down for the Steelers and Maddox was the man for 2003.

I defy you to find another example of a Pro Bowl quarterback and team MVP being treated with such little respect one year after leading his team to the conference championship game.

Maddox was a disaster in 2003 and the Steelers went 6-10.

Stewart went to the Bears and had a horrible year which, in most Steelers fans' eyes, vindicated Bill Cowher and proved that Stewart was a terrible quarterback.

But Mike Ditka knew better. He told Bob Smizik of the Post-Gazette that "It's not Kordell's fault. You can't blame it on him. When he came in, I said he might not be the long-term solution but he might be a short-term remedy. They say he's making bad decisions, well, you make bad decisions when somebody's in your face on every down. I'm not sticking up for him, but Johnny Unitas would have made bad decisions behind that line."

Phil Simms of CBS had been in town and had heard Stewart being bashed on the talk shows. Here's what he wrote for NFL.com: "As I watched the game Monday night, I thought Stewart was the toughest, most competitive, most determined player on the field. And I do not hesitate to say I thought he played extremely hard and showed leadership with his play and his body language. He ran it tough, basically getting no protection. The offense couldn't pick up a blitz, but he just hung in there and made some plays. Whatever hope they had was all hinging on him."

Simms went on to say, "Stewart could play his best year of football this season in Chicago and nobody will know it, with the exception of a few people."

Stewart lasted one year and was run out of Chicago. Of course, so were the head coach and the offensive coordinator, but Stewart was finished as a starting quarterback in the NFL. The quarterbacks who replaced him in Pittsburgh and Chicago and played ahead of him in Baltimore, his last stop, never came close to being as good as he was when he played on a good team for a coach who knew how to use him.

Bill Cowher had ruined his reputation in 1999 and not even an MVP-caliber year in 2001 could change the perception that coaches, fans and media had of him. Cowher made Stewart guilty of being a bad quarterback and he spent the last five years of his career trying to prove himself innocent.

In 2004 Cowher had to be talked into drafting a kid named Ben Roethlisberger in the first round. He was happy with Maddox and wanted to draft an offensive lineman instead of a quarterback. Whatever you think of Stewart, Cowher made it obvious that he was not as good at evaluating the quarterback position as Stewart was at playing it.

Again, two words: Kent Graham.

In 2004, the Baltimore Ravens did the Steelers a favor and knocked Maddox, who had the body and the mobility of an insurance salesman, out of the second game of the season and Cowher was taken kicking and screaming out of the "Tommy Gun Era" and into the "Big Ben Era."

In the final analysis, Kordell Stewart had proven me right for all time. The Steelers could win with him at quarterback.

He might still be playing as I write this in 2010, if not for Bill Cowher.

CHAPTER 28

SHORT STOP
BELL RINGS UP BARRY

think it was 1992. It might have been 1991, but the year doesn't matter. I was in Bradenton, Fla., covering Pirates spring training for KDKA-TV back when covering spring training was still fun and an interesting assignment. Now, if the local stations do decide to go, they send a reporter down for a few days and have him do as many boring, predictable stories as possible so that, for several days after he comes back, they can fool the audience into believing that he's actually still down there covering the Pirates.

In the good old days, we would make two weeklong trips to Brandenton every year, but I digress.

On this day, Bradenton resident "Dickie V" was at McKechnie Field. That would be Dick Vitale, ESPN basketball analyst/clown. He was hanging around the batting cage doing his usual "Dickie V" non-stop, friendly trash-talk, babbling routine and the players were good-naturedly giving it back to him.

Pretty soon, Barry Bonds strolled up to the cage and started showing off for Vitale. It was pretty pathetic. I've always thought that Bonds' biggest problems were a result of something pretty simple.

He's dumb as a rock.

Bonds was trying to get some friendly trash-talking going with his teammates and it wasn't funny and his teammates were ignoring him.

Instead of getting the clue and shutting up, Barry just turned it up a notch. Jay Bell, the Pirates shortstop and most-media-friendly player, was one of the guys trying to get some batting practice in while Bonds continued his unbelievably obnoxious chirping.

Then Barry made a big mistake. He moved from the back of the batting cage behind the plate to the end of the right side of the cage.

He kept chirping and the more unfunny he got the louder he got.

Bell was a good No. 2 hitter, who was very good at hitting the ball to the right side behind the runner. But he also had decent power and could pull the ball. As he was taking his swings, he was alternating between pulling the ball and dropping his right shoulder, doing an inside-out swing and punching the ball to the right side of the infield.

Bonds kept chirping.

I was right behind the cage watching Bell and I saw him drop his right shoulder way down and make an even more pronounced inside-out motion.

Bang.

The ball hit off the bar of the batting stage where Bonds was standing. Bonds was down. The ball had hit him in the face. Fortunately for Bonds and unfortunately for the rest of humanity, the impact was softened by the cage's ropes.

Bonds was looked at by the trainer and got up and left the home plate area with a welt or two on his face.

I was convinced that Bell had done it on purpose.

Fortunately for us, our cameraman, Michael Challik, had the tape rolling at the time. We took the tape back to the truck and watched it several times. The more I watched it the more convinced I was. Bell had great bat control and it was obvious that, on the ball that hit Bonds, he had made a drastic adjustment in his swing that looked totally different from every other swing.

Of course, I couldn't ask Bell if he was trying to hit Bonds to shut him up because he would never admit to it, not even off the record. I never liked talking to Bonds and had no interest in asking him, but I did want an expert second opinion, so I asked the Pirates' third base coach, Rich Donnelly, to take a look at the tape.

Donnelly was (and I'm sure still is) one of those great baseball characters who make hanging around a ballpark enjoyable. He was full of great stories and had a great sense of humor. When I approached him to look at the tape I didn't say that I thought Bell had purposely tried to hit Bonds because I didn't want to influence his opinion. I just said I had a tape that I wanted him to see because I was interested in his reaction.

Donnelly, still in uniform, squeezed himself into our TV truck that was parked down the right field line and we rolled the videotape.

He got a funny look on his face and then said, "Let me see that again." Another funny look and then he said, "One more time."

Donnelly watched the tape again and then a big smile came over his face and, as he was backing out of the truck, he said, "It's been really nice doing business with you guys. Have a nice day."

It was his way of saying, "I know exactly why you wanted me to see that tape and I see exactly what you see, but I'm not saying a word."

And that was that.

The media reported that Bonds had been involved in a scary batting cage "accident" and that he was OK and that it could have been much worse. There were only a few of us who were convinced that it was no accident and we all had a newfound admiration for Jay Bell.

Imagine the effect on baseball history if Bell's "foul" ball had caused damage to Bonds' eye and ended his career before he ever got a chance to juice up.

Wouldn't that have been a shame?

CHAPTER 29

NO

"NO." That was the first word of my Post-Gazette column on Saturday, November 1, 1997. It was three days before election day when voters in 11 Western Pennsylvania counties would be voting on a referendum that asked whether the state should use their money to pay for new stadiums for the Pirates and Steelers.

I was telling my readers how I would be voting and I was urging them to do the same. If there was anybody else in the local sports media who had come out publicly against the funding for the stadiums, I was never aware of it. The general managers of KDKA Radio and KDKA-TV did a duet on television in the days leading up to the election urging viewers to vote yes. It was the only editorial done by a KDKA-TV General Manager in at least 15 years and is still the only time that the radio GM has done an editorial on TV.

That made me a little uncomfortable as I sat down to write my column.

I had lots of press box discussions with my friends in the sports media and officials from both teams and, believe me, I was The Lone Ranger on the issue.

In my more than 30 years working in the Pittsburgh media, standing against forcing the taxpayers to fund stadiums for the Pirates and Steelers was my proudest moment.

I've never been more right.

It had taken me a while to come around to that position.

Back in 1991, Pittsburgh Mayor Sophie Masloff had come out in favor of building a new 44,000 seat ballpark for the Pirates. She said it should be placed on the North Shore near the Sixth Street Bridge and be called Roberto Clemente Stadium.

Everybody laughed at her.

Here is the first sentence of my column in the Post-Gazette the following Saturday: "Sophie Masloff for President."

I had been saying for at least 12 years that Three Rivers Stadium was a dump and that it was killing Pirates attendance. I had even done stories on KDKA-TV suggesting that it was time for a new ballpark patterned after Forbes Field. Over the next few years, new ballparks patterned after old ones were going up all over the country and I had developed the attitude that, if it could be done in other cities, there was no reason it couldn't or shouldn't be done in Pittsburgh.

A trip to the new Camden Yards in Baltimore convinced me even more. The park was beautiful and I saw thousands of people emptying out into the streets of Baltimore after the Orioles game and I thought it was exactly what Pittsburgh needed.

In 1995, the voters of Allegheny County elected two Republican commissioners for the first time in 60 years. That's the way voters are in Allegheny County; they'll keep putting Democrats in power, but they'll only put up with malfeasance, ineptitude and corruption for 50 or 60 years and then, by God, they'll vote 'em out.

Bob Cranmer and Larry Dunn were the Republicans and Mike Dawida was the Democrat. Both Dunn and Cranmer ran on the promise that they would oppose government funding for stadiums.

Dawida worked hard to change their minds and eventually Cranmer did change his. He turned his back on Dunn and the people who voted him into office and joined forces with Dawida.

Before Cranmer had changed his mind and decided it was OK to use taxpayer money for the stadiums, I had run into Dawida on the street outside the Allegheny County Court House following a press conference. I said, "Look, Baltimore did it. Cleveland did it. Chicago did it. Why can't Pittsburgh do it? We always have reasons why we can't do anything around here. Just do it."

He agreed but said he was in the minority among the county commissioners and there was only so much he could do.

A few months later, I ran into Dawida again and he told me that he had told Cranmer of our conversation that day and he said Cranmer was swayed by my "Just do it" argument.

If that's true, it's pretty scary. It's one thing for a reporter on a rant to say "Just do it" and quite another for an elected official to actually betray the people who voted for him by "just doing it."

I was being swayed in the opposite direction, first, by my brother, Bill, the libertarian. He had been pumping me with information about how the promises of new revenues produced by ballparks in other cities were never fulfilled. I continued to use my Camden Yards argument until I found out that the situation in Baltimore was much different from the situation in Pittsburgh.

Taxpayers weren't being forced to pay for new buildings for the Orioles and Ravens. Lottery ticket buyers were paying for them.

Voluntarily.

I called the Maryland Sports Authority and was told that they raised more money than they needed for the stadiums and the surplus was going to fund education. I'm sure that there are some tax dollars involved somewhere but what was important to me was that the vast majority of the money came from people who had the option of not buying a lottery ticket if they didn't like the idea of their money going to team owners who should have to pay for their own buildings.

The fine citizens of Western Pennsylvania weren't going to have that option. Government leaders gave no consideration whatsoever to using a lottery to fund the stadiums.

Pretty soon I moved firmly into the "NO" column.

My media friends couldn't understand why I would be opposed to new stadiums for the Pirates and the Steelers. Andy Sheehan, a reporter at KDKA, told me I was cutting my own throat.

Kevin McClatchy had formed a group to buy the Pirates in September of 1995 and within a few weeks, the National League informed the city that the deal would not be approved without a promise of a new ballpark.

The papers, radio and TV were filled with horror stories about the Pirates moving out of town. It was at the same time in 1995 that Dan

Rooney sent a chill through the Steeler Nation by saying that the Steelers couldn't remain competitive unless they got a new stadium.

Keep in mind that it was in the middle of all the horror stories and predictions of Pittsburgh without it's football and baseball teams in 1995 that the citizens of Allegheny County, for the first time in 60 years, voted for two Republican commissioners, both of whom campaigned on the promise of no tax money for stadiums.

It would be two years of threats and promises before it would finally be put to a vote.

I remember sitting at home on the Sunday morning before the 1997 election watching a live town hall meeting on WTAE. Dan Rooney was there to plead his case to the crowd. He talked about the overtime win over Jacksonville the week before and how wonderful it made everybody feel and he asked them to imagine what it would be like without the Steelers.

I could have puked.

I thought, "Yeah, Dan, the Steelers are woven into the fabric of Pittsburgh. Millions of people live and die with them. That's why you're a multi-gazillionaire. You've built a really good business. Why should these people be forced to give their money to you?"

The Steelers were worth about $350 million in 1997. In 2010 they're worth about $1 billion. Heinz Field played a major role in the Steelers tripling in value.

My uncle, Larry Hatch, opened a restaurant back in 1949 called Eat 'n Park. It worked out pretty well for him. His restaurants are as much a part of the local culture as the Steelers. They've created millions of dollars in tax revenue and employed thousands of people. Would he have been justified in asking the local politicians to force the local citizens to pay for the construction of a new warehouse or a few more restaurants?

"NO" won by a landslide. The final score was 530,706 to 281,336. That's 65-35. How many times have you seen an election that lopsided?

Reagan only beat Mondale 58-42 in 1984.

It wasn't just "NO." It was a resounding "NO."

Of course, our local leaders accepted the will of the people and directed their efforts toward finding private funding for the Steelers and told the Pirates to get out of town and come back when they played in a league that gives them a chance to compete.

Sure they did.

Within a week a new plan emerged. It would be known as "Plan B" and would involve taking money from an already existing pile of taxpayer money and giving it to the Steelers and Pirates. The criminals who foisted this monstrosity on the public would tell you, even to this day and with a straight face, that they didn't go against the will of the people because the people had said no to *new* taxes. Every politician who pushed the new plan knew that the voters would have gone 65-35 against it, too, if they had been given a chance.

Western Pennsylvania taxpayers had made it abundantly clear that they were opposed to their money being used to build new facilities for the Pirates and Steelers and the politicians made it abundantly clear that they were going to ignore the wishes of the people who pay their salaries.

A Pennsylvania Poll showed 55 percent opposed to Plan B, 32 percent in favor and 13 percent unsure.

The Regional Asset District (RAD) controlled the money that was proposed for the stadiums and it had to sign off on it before the Steelers and Pirates got their money. There were seven board members and six had to vote in favor in order for the money to be allocated. It became apparent that there were only five votes in favor.

So, the politicians — after seeing the idea voted down 65-35 and seeing the polls showing the taxpayers opposed to Plan B, and after seeing that the duly appointed RAD board didn't have enough votes — gave up and decided to devote their time to trying to find private funding.

Uh, no they didn't.

They got Fred Baker to resign from the board. Fred had been appointed by Bob Cranmer. You remember him. He's the Republican County Commissioner who had been elected by promising no tax money for stadiums. Baker was replaced by David Christopher, who can go to his grave knowing that his yes vote cost the taxpayers of Allegheny County about $350 million.

You want to know something? If the vote were held today, even with the two facilities shining brightly on the North Shore, it would still be 65-35 against. It might even be more lopsided.

I moved to Washington County in 1990 , so I pay a six percent sales tax compared to seven percent in Allegheny County. That doesn't mean I haven't helped to pay the mortgages on Heinz Field and PNC Park. Some of my state taxes are in there somewhere and everybody in the country pays part of their federal taxes to fund stadiums thousands of miles away.

But who cares? It's not like we're over taxed or anything.

If you live in Allegheny County and buy a $30,000 car, you pay $300 more than I pay for the same car in Washington County. And a good portion of that extra $300 goes to pay for Heinz Field and PNC Park.

I can't tell you how much I appreciate your contribution to making the Steelers and Pirates more competitive. Especially the Pirates.

CHAPTER 30

SHORT STOP
TOO MANY 50-ISH WHITE GUYS

NOT long after I left WTAE in 1985, I was sitting in the Penguins' press box next to John Clendenon, the executive sports editor of the Pittsburgh Post-Gazette. He told me that he had enjoyed my radio commentaries on "The O'Brien and Gary Show" on WTAE and 96 KIX and asked me if I had ever considered writing a newspaper column.

I said that I hadn't, mainly because I always got the feeling that newspaper people looked down their noses at microphone pukes. (That's what my boss with the Lafayette Drillers used to call radio announcers. I always thought it was a good description.)

Clendenon asked me to write a sample "notes" column and he said he would look it over. A notes column is the easiest column to write because it's mostly stream of consciousness.

Kind of like this book.

He read my little sample and told me that it was "the quintessential notes column." Being an ignorant microphone puke, it took me a second or two to realize that he was telling me that he liked it a lot.

So I wrote a column for the Post-Gazette for 12 of the next 13 years. One of the advantages of working in TV, while you're also working in radio or writing for a newspaper, is that your face is a walking advertisement and it's also a great magnet for feedback.

Nothing I've done in my more than 30 years in the Pittsburgh media got me a more positive response than my P-G column.

In October of 1998, I got a call from the P-G's sports editor, Fritz Huysman. He told me that, for budgetary reasons, he had been told to eliminate all freelance columnists. The success of my column had led to other microphone pukes getting columns in local newspapers and that included Stan Savran, who shared the Saturday sports opinion page with me.

Stan got the axe, too.

Huysmann told me that he could keep me on for less money but that he wouldn't want to insult me with the amount that the paper would allow him to pay.

So, I was finished at the Post-Gazette. No big deal. Happens all the time.

Here's what was a big deal to me: I was told that the paper's top editor — I think his official title was Editor in Cheese — John Craig, had said, out loud, in the very recent past, that the Post-Gazette sports pages were populated by too many 50-ish white guys.

I was about three weeks from turning 50 when I got the word. I had also been white for as long as I could remember and was pretty sure I still was. I wouldn't have cared that much if not for the fact that Craig was an officious, pompous snob who oversaw a newspaper that liked to present itself as progressive and diverse and here he was getting rid of somebody (maybe two people, since Savran was guilty of the same offenses) because he was a little too old and a little too white.

I figured it was worth a mention on the air.

That didn't go over well with KDKA management and I was almost fired. I would have been fine with that because I was already tired of working there and would have enjoyed the large severance check, but I survived. I also would have had a lot of fun telling that story to Bill O'Reilly and Sean Hannity.

KDKA and the Post-Gazette had a news gathering partnership that, to this day, neither knows how to take advantage of and I had apparently created some tension there.

I knew I was putting out a good column every week and I was proven right when, in less than two days, I signed up seven local papers to carry it.

That was 12 years ago.

I'm sure that, since then, you've enjoyed reading the diversified comments from the P-G's Muslim sports columnist and all their black and Hispanic sportswriters, not to mention the Native Americans and dwarves who have been providing a rainbow of opinions since then.

The two sports columnists now working for the Post-Gazette are Gene Collier and Ron Cook, both excellent writers, but if you scoured North America for a year you couldn't find two whiter, more 50-ish men.

CHAPTER 31

THANKS FOR THE MAMMARIES

HERE'S a list, off the top of my head, of competitive sports that I'm 99.9 percent sure were invented by a man:

Football	Baseball	Basketball
Hockey	Golf	Rugby
Soccer	Tennis	Badminton
Boxing	Bowling	Wrestling
Fencing	Billiards	Lacrosse
Polo	Skeet shooting	Archery
Skiing	Swimming	Diving
Squash	Racquetball	Pole Vaulting
Long Jumping	Sprinting	Cricket

Here's a list of the competitive sports that I'm pretty sure were invented by a woman:

Jacks	Hopscotch

So, as politically incorrect as it may be to say, women are Joanie-come-latelies when it comes to sports, not only in America but worldwide.

Now, I'm no anthropologist, but I'm pretty sure that we (men and women) have been on the planet an equal amount of time. Why is it, then, that a woman (as far as I know and I'm open to any corrections on my list) has yet to come up with a competitive activity that men are interested in playing?

Where have you ladies been?

And, by the way, I'm conceding you jacks and hopscotch, but they also could very well have been invented by a man and no real man would be interested in playing either "sport," anyway.

Could it be that all these sports were created by men because men were looking for a way to get away from their wives?

What we now know as golf began in the 12th century in Scotland, when shepherds started using sticks to knock stones into rabbit holes on the current site of the Royal and Ancient Golf Club of St. Andrews.

How do you think the womenfolk felt about that?

Do you think they thought the men were being ridiculous?

Do you think they were feeling cheated because they weren't invited to play?

What would the reaction have been if one of the guys in that first foursome of shepherds back in 1100-something had asked the other three if they would mind if he brought his wife along?

They would have pounded *him* into a rabbit hole.

With all due respect to women everywhere, I think the shepherds were hoping that their wives would continue to think they were insane for trying to knock stones into rabbit holes because it assured them of getting away from them for a few hours.

If you go all the way back to the first Olympics, it's safe to say that it took women about 2,500 years to figure out that men were on to something.

Again, ladies, what took you so long?

Is there an anthropological explanation for this?

You have to give women credit, though. After giving men a 2,500-year head start, they seem to be holding down about half the jobs on America's top sports networks.

They not only discovered the joy of playing sports, they discovered that they can be paid lots of money for talking about it.

As long as they don't look like Beano Cook.

Or John Clayton.

Picture John Clayton's identical twin sister standing on the sideline on ESPN's "Monday Night Football" telecast.

How about a woman who looks like Beano Cook co-anchoring "Sportscenter"?

Has anything set back the advancement of women in the workplace more than women sportscasters?

You'll know that a woman is working for a national TV network because of her knowledge of sports when you see one who looks like Dan Dierdorf.

Suzy Kolber is still cute as a button at 45, but will ESPN still want her on the sideline when she's 55?

Chris Berman brags about losing 40 pounds on Nutrisystem but he still weighs at least 80 pounds more than any woman who will ever sit on an ESPN studio set. Picture for a moment getting your scores and highlights from a 50-something woman who's built like Chris Berman.

Ain't gonna happen.

It doesn't matter what their journalistic credentials are or how extensive their athletic backgrounds may be, the vast majority of women doing sports for ESPN and other networks are there for one reason.

Eye candy.

That's not to say that many of them don't do a good job, but I'll let you in on a little secret.

It ain't that tough.

You sit or stand in the studio and read a Teleprompter. Women do it every day at local news stations around the country. The fact that what they're reading in the Teleprompter is sports news instead of news that may actually matter, doesn't make it any more difficult.

You might think that any sportscaster would kill to be a "Sportscenter" anchor. I can't think of a sportscasting job that could be more boring.

Trust me. There's nothing glamorous about sitting in a cubicle in Bristol, Connecticut, on a Tuesday night in late August, preparing to read a Teleprompter and do the voice-over of highlights of a Royals-Indians game. They never get to see a game in person. It's the perfect job for someone who is more interested in being on TV than actually going to games and covering sports. And that makes it a perfect job for a person whose Number One purpose is to provide the eye candy.

That's why you see so many women popping up on ESPN and the other sports networks.

And, again, no matter how many they hire, you'll never see one who looks like John Madden.

It's really no different from someone hiring a secretary because her appearance will brighten up the office.

I understand that their good looks don't disqualify them, either. Nor should they. The point is that many men are being bumped out of jobs only because they don't have mammary glands, but nobody has the guts to say so.

Consider it said.

There are lots of women doing sideline reporting who seem to have, at the very least, a working knowledge of the sport they're covering and do a good job of relaying information up to the booth.

Again, not a tough job and in most cases unnecessary.

ABC actually put Lisa Gurerro on the "Monday Night Football" sideline in 2003. As a sports reporter, Lisa had really nice breasts, but there she was holding down a job once held by Lynn Swann.

Of course, Swann was replaced on the "Monday Night" sideline in 1998 by Leslie Visser, a female sportscaster pioneer who, despite never having said anything worth repeating, funny or insightful, has worked as a network sportscaster for 30 years and is the only woman in the Pro Football Hall of Fame.

A man who was as vapid as she has been allowed to be on network TV for more than 30 years wouldn't last 20 minutes.

Visser has a strong athletic and journalistic background and always did a solid, professional job but only someone trying to over-estimate the impact of women in sportscasting would suggest that she was ever anything more than a run-of-the-mill sportscaster.

I guess my point is that way too many ordinary talents are elevated to prominent positions based solely on their appearance and then some are passed off as worthy of being mentioned in the same breath as Heywood Hale Broun or Howard Cosell.

It would be a lot more honest if the play-by-play announcer would throw it to the sideline reporter by saying, "We haven't checked in on

Suzy for a while, let's go down to the sideline and get another look at those fabulous breasts. Suzy, what'ya got?"

Feminists should be picketing ESPN everyday for its sexist policy of only hiring (with very few exceptions) hot looking women. Instead, everybody just pretends to believe that these former models, cheerleaders and actresses were hired because of their in-depth knowledge of sports and their amazing journalistic skills.

They were hired because network executives are convinced that most men couldn't possibly be tuning in to just watch the *game*. They know men think about sex every 12 seconds and they're convinced that we'll tune out of the football game and go to Cinemax unless we know that there is a possibility that we'll see some cleavage every couple of minutes.

Maybe I run with a bad crowd, but I have never heard a man comment on a female sportscaster's insightful comment or funny line. And I mean never. I've heard lots of men discuss which female sportscaster has the prettiest face or the nicest body part and I have a feeling that most of the female sportscasters applied for the jobs they have because they knew their appearance was enough to get them hired. I really don't think a hot chick makes it any more likely that a guy is going to tune into "Sportscenter." If they're that desperate to see the female form, there are plenty of pictures of pretty girls available on their computer. We had several young women work as interns in the KDKA sports department who said they wanted to be TV sportscasters and I can assure you that not one of them looked like Trey Wingo.

It would be interesting to track the career paths of some of the top female network sports announcers to see how many of them followed the traditional route of working in a small or micro-market covering high school sports and worked their way up the ladder to the big time. Virtually every man you see doing sports on national TV got his start at a small station somewhere. The play-by-play guys started doing high school games and worked their way up. How many hot looking, future network sportscastrerettes do you suppose are doing high school football or basketball play-by-play these days? You can be sure there are lots and lots of guys doing it and some of them will never be considered for a network job because they don't have the right plumbing.

I don't think someone who reports on a sport has to have played it at some level, but I would like to feel confident that someone expressing an opinion on football would have at least juked somebody out once.

Can you picture Leslie Visser juking somebody out?

Think she has ever tried to catch a football while trying to keep two feet in bounds? How about short-hopping a line drive?

Don't get me wrong, I've come across a lot of men who, in my mind, disqualified themselves from reporting on any sport involving running or throwing.

I knew a good sports columnist in Lafayette, Louisiana, who worked as official scorer for the Lafayette Drillers of the Texas League in 1975. I always thought he was a good writer but, when I was doing the radio play-by-play of Drillers games, I would often question his rulings.

So would the players. They were known to respond to seeing "ERROR" go up on the scoreboard, after one of their teammates failed to make what would have been a spectacular play, by waving towels toward the press box.

It happened a lot.

A couple of months into the season, prior to a Drillers game, the Drillers' staff played a softball game against the media.

The columnist, whose name I've forgotten, made it clear why he had a tough time telling the difference between an error and a base hit.

He couldn't throw a ball 12 feet and he had hands like feet.

It was so bad that, if I had been sports editor and seen that, he would have never covered another baseball game.

I was no world-class athlete. Far from it, but I could play a little bit. When I worked for minor league baseball teams, I made a point to put on a uniform every once in a while and shag fly balls during batting practice. I didn't expect them to beg the manager to sign me up. I just wanted them to know that I had made an over-the-shoulder catch at least once in my life. It may not have mattered to them, but it was important to me that they knew the guy who was talking about them every night on the radio knew a good play when he saw one because he had made a few himself.

When I was 35 years old and had been on ice skates once in my life, I decided to teach myself how to skate. I got to be a good enough skater to play in some pathetic pick-up games and did a good job of embarrassing myself, but I know that I also got a much better appreciation for what goes into being a good hockey player.

A real turn-off for me is a female anchor on "Sportscenter" who insists on voicing-over the highlights like a man. Maybe it's a generational thing and I'm showing my age, but I can't get used to hearing a woman say, "And then, top nine, we're tied at 3 and A-Rod goes yard."

There are times when a female voice just doesn't sound right.

Imagine Leslie Visser saying this: "There are 27 teams in the National Football League and then … there are the Pittsburgh Steelers."

That's the opening line of the Steelers' 1979 highlight film, "A Cut Above." John Facenda created a lot more drama than Leslie or any other female voice would have.

How about Hannah Storm instead of Howard Cosell saying, "Down goes Frazier! Down goes Frazier! Down goes Frazier!"

Just wouldn't work.

With apologies to Pam Ward of ESPN, I can't handle a female voice doing the play-by-play of a college football game. She does a perfectly respectable job of calling the action, but when I hear her voice I have to go for the mute button.

Sorry.

I wouldn't be surprised if Pam could beat me to a bloody pulp, but I'd also be willing to bet that she's never juked anybody out.

Getting back to where we started with the shepherds in Scotland, although most men would never admit it, I think most of us liked it a lot better when women wondered why any human would be interested in watching another human try to knock a rock into a rabbit hole.

WHILE WE'RE ON THE SUBJECT

Just in case I've just convinced you that I'm a male chauvinist pig who thinks women should be kept barefoot, pregnant and standing by the stove, when I was doing my general-topic talk show on KDKA radio, I was one of the first people in the country to say that Sarah Palin should be John McCain's running mate. And it had nothing to do with her looks. I read her life story and saw her accomplishments in Alaska and immediately became one of her biggest fans. If she ran against Barack Obama for president tomorrow, I would vote for her.

But she's also a former sportscaster and I wouldn't want to hear her do the play-by-play of the Ohio State-Michigan game.

I have no issues with powerful women and I don't think any woman should be told that any job is a man's job. They should be given every opportunity to compete for any job they want. And, as I'm sure the lovely Betty Friedan would tell you, it should have nothing to do with their appearance.

CHAPTER 32

SHORT STOP
KISSING MICHELLE PFEIFFER

I made the decision in the summer of 1971 to go to summer school at Kent State. By then, I knew that the most important thing for me was to get experience at the campus radio station and I figured that there would be very little competition for jobs.

I was right.

I got the job of doing afternoon sportscasts on WKSU-FM, a station with about a 60-mile radius that had listeners in the Youngstown, Akron and Cleveland markets because it featured a lot of classical music and jazz. I took a few classes, did a five-minute sportscast every day and took advantage of the ridiculous number of bars in Kent, Ohio, at night.

A friend of mine from Pittsburgh introduced me to a kid from Kennedy Township, who was doing the same thing that I was doing, only he was a drama major who was hoping to take advantage of less competition for roles in the Kent State summer theater.

His name was Mike Douglas and he was a typical Pittsburgh guy — very funny, loved sports and looking to have a good time at night. He and I and a couple of other guys from Pittsburgh hung out quite a bit that summer and had a lot of laughs. We hung out a little more the following year and hitchhiked home to Pittsburgh together a few times.

Mike went his way and I went mine and we lost contact after we both left Kent State in 1972.

Michael Keaton with Paul and me the night in 1988 that "Batman"
premiered in Pittsburgh. Michael came disguised as Bruce Wayne.

One night in late 1976 or early 1977, I happened to walk by the TV
and see Mike in a scene with Bernadette Peters. It was a sitcom called "All's
Fair" that also starred Richard Crenna.

I said to my wife, "Hey, I know that guy. It's Mike Douglas."

It turned out that he used to be Mike Douglas.

He had changed his name to Michael Keaton.

Flash forward to the early '90s. I'm sitting in the Three Rivers Stadium
press box covering a Pirates' playoff game and someone from the Pirates
tells me that there is a guy outside who wants to talk to me.

It was Michael Keaton. I had run into him several times since I saw
him on TV, usually at major sporting events involving Pittsburgh teams.

He asked me to come with him to a private box where he was watching
the game with his brothers and a bunch of nieces and nephews. While
we're walking from the press box to his suite, he says, "Man this is great.
You get paid to come to these games. The Pirates now, a few months ago
the Penguins. What a great job."

Then he paused the way only a guy who used to do standup comedy
could do and he said. "Of course, I have a pretty good job, too. I spent all
day yesterday kissing Michelle Pfeiffer."

Summer school had paid off pretty well for both of us.

GUNG HO

I became a movie star myself in 1985. I starred in a picture with Michael Keaton called "Gung Ho." OK, I didn't star in it. I had a small part. OK, I didn't have a small part. I was an extra. But I was a really important extra.

"Gung Ho" is the story of a Pennsylvania auto plant that is close to going out of business until it is saved by a group of Japanese auto experts who come over and rescue it.

Keaton plays the guy who's in charge of convincing the Japanese to come over and show the Americans how to turn the factory around. My scene took place in a supermarket where the girlfriend of Keaton's character (played by Mimi Rogers) works.

Keaton is visiting her at the market when the company gets word that the Japanese have agreed to help. A young guy, looking for Keaton's character to tell him the news, comes sprinting through the front door of the store (which was a since-closed grocery store in Wilkinsburg), cuts around the cash registers and then runs into an old lady pushing a shopping cart.

I'm the guy in the cereal aisle who does a double take as the guy comes running by. I added the little flinch myself and the director, Ron Howard, actually told me that he liked it.

I'm still waiting to hear from him for my first starring role.

The actor was Jihmi Kennedy, a good character actor who has been in a lot of movies, including the Civil War movie "Glory." After the scene, he came up to me and said, "We had a little moment there."

I had no idea what he meant, although I do remember making eye contact with him as he came flying around the cash registers. I pretended that I knew exactly what he was talking about, figuring he'd respect me more as an actor.

I learned a lot about the movie business. We did at least 10 takes and, with set-up time, it took several hours to shoot that one little scene.

A few days later, I used my connections to hook the cast and crew up with tickets to a Springsteen concert at Three Rivers Stadium. Keaton paid me for his tickets but Howard apparently thought I had gotten them for free and he still owes me.

When I get really desperate, I'm planning on calling him and demanding that he give me a major role in his next film.

I figure he's gotta remember the flinch.

CHAPTER 33

THE SOFT BIGOTRY OF LOW EXPECTATIONS

IT was January, 1983, and the Pitt basketball team had just lost a close game in Landover, Maryland, to the great Georgetown team that included Patrick Ewing. I was doing the color for the WTAE telecast and I was sitting at the press table listening on my headset as play-by-play man Bill Hillgrove interviewed Pitt's best player, Clyde Vaughn, underneath the basket to my left.

Hillgrove said to Vaughn that, although Pitt would have loved to have won the game, the team had to be happy with the way it played on the road against such a tough opponent. Here's what Vaughn, a nice kid and by all accounts a good student, said:

"Yes we is Mr. Hillgrove."

This was a college senior who was month or two from graduating from the University of Pittsburgh and he said, "Yes we is." Hillgrove didn't laugh and neither did the cameraman and I doubt that anybody who was associated with the Pitt program did a double-take.

I almost fell out of my chair.

"Yes we is"?

Imagine if a white kid had said that.

Even if you don't remember Vaughn, you knew he was black as soon as you read the quote, didn't you?

And as you're reading this, you may be feeling a little uncomfortable for me because you think I'm treading in dangerous territory. I'm risking being called a racist.

When I heard Vaughn's answer, I remember thinking, "I wonder if the head of the English department at Pitt is watching and, if so, how he's reacting." I also remember thinking how there was no excuse for Vaughn, who was the face of the Pitt basketball program and was a frequent representative of the university because of his star stature, to speak like that in front of tens of thousands of people in Western Pennsylvania. He had been at Pitt for four years and had done dozens of TV and radio interviews and just about every one of them was heard by somebody associated with the Pitt program.

Here we are, a generation later, and the situation isn't any better and may actually be worse.

The problem, of course, was that Vaughn was black and less is expected of black players when it comes to being articulate.

If a white reporter dares to admit to noticing that a black player is articulate, he risks being labeled a racist.

The NCAA has rules that prevent universities from giving athletes formal training in how to deal with the media because the NCAA has rules for everything, but, in this case, it's because it would mean that athletes are getting benefits that are not offered to the rest of the student body.

Of course, the rest of the student body doesn't bring in millions of dollars for the university and isn't asked to do too many TV interviews, but the NCAA, despite the fact that it is made up of institutions of higher learning, is pretty stupid.

Ninety-nine percent of the kids who play college basketball don't go on to play professionally. Don't the schools that exploit these kids by making millions of dollars from their performances owe it to them to see that they're prepared for life after basketball?

Notice I said life after basketball, not life after college.

The graduation rates for top-50 college basketball programs tell you that most of the kids getting scholarships don't take advantage of them. They are basketball players first and students second.

It used to be and is still supposed to be the other way around.

And the nerds who represent the NCAA at the men's basketball tournament never refer to the players as players when speaking about them to the media. They're always "student athletes."

What a joke.

Kids who play in major media markets like Pittsburgh should be shown how to take advantage of the media exposure and use it to open doors when their college careers are over.

What does a potential employer think when he hears "Yes we is"?

Would you consider, for one minute, hiring somebody who said, "Yes we is"?

"Hello, PNC Bank, Mr. Vaughn speaking, may I help you? Are we an all-purpose bank? Yes, we is."

CLICK.

Nobody who says "Yes we is" would work for me in any position that required dealing with the public. Just as nobody who says "Yinz" would ever work for me.

"Hello, State Farm Insurance, Mr. Steigerwald speaking. May I help you? OK, how long have yinz lived in the home?

CLICK.

I guarantee you that, if a white kid dropped a "yinz" in a press conference or an interview, there would be laughter from the media, the university would be embarrassed and the kid would be told that he probably shouldn't use that word anymore.

Even today, a black kid saying "Yes we is" would hardly be noticed much less laughed at or corrected. Pitt could hold a post-game press conference with three black players and one white player and all three black players could "we was" it all the way through and nobody would notice. If the white kid dropped one "we was," everybody in the room would notice because black kids aren't expected to speak proper English. White kids are.

I can't tell you how many times I've sat in press conferences and watched college kids — mostly black — butcher the English language.

Some of them made up for sounding like they were speaking a foreign language by wearing their baseball cap sideways or pulled down over their ears.

I used to sit there trying to imagine the kid writing an English composition or answering an essay question.

Or showing up for a job interview.

I realize it's a cultural thing, but as America's Smartest Man — economist/philosopher/black man Thomas Sowell — always says, "Culture has consequences."

I also used to wonder how coaches and college Sports Information Directors could watch the performance of their kids in press conferences and not do something to correct it.

That's also a cultural thing.

It's called "the soft bigotry of low expectations."

Black kids just aren't expected to be as articulate as white kids.

Now *that's* racist but it's also obviously what most of the white coaches and administrators think or they would do a better job of correcting it.

The kids who do go on to the NBA and NFL end up speaking the same way and representing their schools to even more people. I often wonder how the teachers at their universities feel when they see one of their former students "We was-ing" his way through a national TV interview.

It would be jarring to hear a white kid speak that way.

NFL locker rooms are full of guys who spent four years or more on a college campus and don't speak English as well as former Penguin, Ruslan Fedotenko, who grew up in Russia. And, believe me, it was always jarring to hear a really well-spoken black star athlete. Don't kid yourself, everybody in the sports media notices when an NBA or NFL player "talks white." They won't say it out loud, but they notice and that's a shame.

College coaches and administrators talk all the time about how important it is for their athletes to perform well in the classroom and graduate, but they drop the ball when they allow a kid to spend four years on a college campus without helping him do a better job of presenting himself to the public.

One reason is that they are afraid of being called racist for suggesting that a black kid do a better job of enunciating or expanding his vocabulary, but mostly it's because there's a prevailing attitude that black kids shouldn't be expected to speak well.

Again, the soft bigotry of low expectations.

There's also another obvious reason. There are way too many kids taking up space on college campuses who have no business being there. That last sentence could also be translated by some to be code for "There are too many black kids playing college football and basketball," but that's not it at all. There are too many kids who don't qualify as college students using scholarship money that could be going to kids who might actually take advantage of a free education.

It might also be a little racist to assume that by saying there are good student athletes being deprived of the opportunity to play major college football or basketball, you're only talking about white kids.

Believe it or not, there are black kids who are good athletes and real college material. For every black kid who runs a 4.4-forty, reads at the fourth-grade level and has a scholarship from a major university, there are probably two or three black kids who run 4.7-forties, graduated from high school with 4.0 grade-point-averages and are playing wide receiver at Bethany or Mount Union instead of West Virginia or Ohio State. Black kids and white kids who have just about as much chance of ending up in the NBA or the NFL as the stars who don't belong anywhere near a classroom, are deprived of the opportunity of playing major college football or basketball. How many 6'10" kids who owed points on their SAT are getting those one-year basketball scholarships at major schools at the expense of a 6'6" kid — black or white — who's majoring in pre-med at a Division II school?

The major programs aren't going to fix the problem by telling coaches to only recruit kids who would be going to college if they didn't play football or basketball. They have boosters and alumni to please and you please them a lot more with nice bowl trips and Elite Eight trips than you do with medical school scholarships.

Forget the ridiculous suggestion that kids be paid to play college football without having to be students. It's supposed to be college kids playing football. Not football players pretending they're students.

You want to get football players ready for the NFL and basketball players ready for the NBA?

Start a minor league.

Nobody ever asked Mario Lemiuex or Sidney Crosby what they scored on the SAT. Their ability to play professional hockey had nothing to do with their understanding of trigonometry or Chaucer. Both the NBA and the NFL, with their age requirements, do their best to force kids who aren't college material to take scholarships away from athletes who are.

Forget the NCAA, too.

It's a bloated bureaucracy that has outlived its usefulness. The NCAA should step aside and let the college presidents decide who's going to represent their university to the world. If a college president doesn't care if the kid playing quarterback has trouble reading "The Cat in the Hat," then bring him in and give him a helmet. A college president shouldn't need the threat of probation to discourage him from allowing kids who can't spell football to get a "scholarship" for playing it.

CHAPTER 34

MISTER ROGERS OR THE STOOGES

MISTER Rogers was like Trix. He was for kids. But nobody ever said Trix were good for kids. And nobody ever said Mister Rogers wasn't good for kids. I've always had my doubts. Not about Trix, about Mister Rogers. Maybe there have been doubts raised about Mister Rogers in other parts of the country, but not in Pittsburgh. Not in Mister Rogers' neighborhood.

He's one famous Pittsburgher I never met and I've never heard anybody say a bad word about him — no stories about him saying, when the tape stopped rolling, "Will somebody tell those little bastards to shut up." Nothing like that. I have no doubt that he was a good person and that he meant well. And I'm sure he had and continues to have a positive influence on kids all over the world.

But he made me nervous.

Well, actually, the idea of my son watching him made me nervous. Let's say you're in the market for a baby-sitter for your 5-year-old-son and your next door neighbor says, "I have the perfect guy for you."

I don't know about you but my first response would be, "Guy?"

And your neighbor says, "Yeah, trust me. He's just a guy who really loves little kids. He runs a day care center. Your son will love him."

You decide to pay Mister Rogers a visit and you're sitting in his living room when he comes in and says. "Hello neighbor," takes off his baby-blue cardigan sweater, sits down, takes off his shoes and puts on a pair of sneakers that no self-respecting man would be caught dead in and pulls out a bunch of puppets. It becomes obvious to you right away that this guy really, really enjoys playing with puppets. It also becomes obvious to you that this guy is a major-league sissy.

Would you really want your kid to hang around with this guy for more than five minutes?

Are you still allowed to refer someone as a sissy?

If not, I blame Mister Rogers.

Please notice that I said Mister Rogers, not Fred Rogers. Fred has made more positive contributions to society than I could ever hope to make and he's a better person than I could ever hope to be. My problem is with the character—Mister Rogers.

It's just that, when I was growing up, if a guy pranced around in girly sneakers, talked like a girl and played with puppets, he was a sissy.

If that doesn't qualify you as a sissy in the 21st century, again, I blame Mister Rogers. Effeminate men have not only become acceptable, they're celebrated and, I'm sorry, but millions of young boys watching Mister Rogers had to have something to do with that. Can you imagine a woman who is as masculine as Mister Rogers was feminine lasting 50 years as a TV role model for kids? Picture a woman with a butch haircut coming in the door, saying, "Hey, how's it hangin' kids?" and then taking off her leather biker jacket, flinging it across a chair, sitting down, slipping on a pair of combat boots, putting on boxing gloves and starting to hit a heavy bag.

Would the idea of this person spending an hour a day with your daughter make you nervous?

That's how I felt about my son or my nephews watching Mister Rogers.

Given a choice, I always preferred the Three Stooges.

I think I was a little too old by the time Mister Rogers came along, although I do have vague memories of watching Josie Carey on WQED and there were puppets. I don't remember what kind of shoes she wore but I'm pretty sure they weren't combat boots.

I am proud to say that it was my generation that was responsible for the great Three Stooges come back. I remember my dad coming home from work one day and telling me to turn on Channel 4 if I wanted to get a good laugh. It was Paul Shannon's "Adventure Time" and he had come up with the brilliant idea of making the Stooges' short features an integral part of his show.

The show was a huge hit and created a nationwide Three Stooges revival.

Let's pause here to contemplate someone trying this in 2010.

Let's say the Three Stooges never existed. The kids cable network, Nickelodeon, introduces a new afternoon show that features three guys who spend 90 per cent of their time on camera inflicting pain on each other with various household items including power tools.

Would anybody be laughing?

Actually the boys (and men) would be laughing. The girls (and women) and the sissies wouldn't get it. Of course it would never last five minutes on the air. Imagine the outrage on all the cable news shows.

Call me crazy but I'm not convinced that the Stooges' message wasn't better than Mister Rogers'. The Stooges never had a happy ending. They always paid a heavy price for their stupidity and I think parents in the '50s did a good job of making it clear to their kids that Moe wasn't really gouging Curly's eyes out and that they shouldn't try to do what the Stooges do anymore than they should try to leap tall buildings in a single bound, change the course of mighty rivers or think that they could create a secret identity and fool a building full of newspaper reporters by putting on a pair of glasses.

Pittsburgh should be proud of Fred Rogers. He's an immortal TV icon but most real men would be more comfortable with their son if he acted more like Moe Howard.

OK, maybe not Moe Howard. How about another guy who used to be on opposite "Mister Roger's Neighborhood."

Popeye.

Now there's a role model for 21st century kids. He fights to the finach 'cause he eats his spinach. He even has a tattoo.

Just like mom.

WHILE WE'RE ON THE SUBJECT

I feel obligated, as a journalist, to say something here about my colleagues at The Daily Planet. Let's take a look at the job that the paper does in its coverage of Superman.

Their best reporter, Lois Lane, has been rescued countless times by Superman, including many, many times when he has swooped her up in his arms and carried her away from danger. So, Lois has been up close and personal with "The Man of Steel."

Superman does most of his work in Metropolis, a huge city with millions of people and lots of media. His face has been splashed everywhere. But, when this guy puts on a pair of glasses and shows up at The Daily Planet to work as mild-mannered reporter Clark Kent, nobody recognizes him as Superman.

The paper's best reporter, Lois, goes out on assignments with this guy, rides in the same car. Clark disappears every time Superman shows up, but Lois, despite her many years in investigative reporting, never makes the connection. Nor does the editor of The Daily Planet, Perry White, or an entire building full of highly trained journalists.

The cops and detectives, whose bacon he has saved over the years, see Clark Kent hanging around the crime scene every day and they've had up-close-and-personal moments with Superman, yet it never occurs to them that they look amazingly alike.

It would be different if Superman had the power to alter his face. You know, stretch his nose, make his ears bigger, change the color of his eyes. He does it by putting on a pair of black-framed glasses.

Picture Ben Roethlisberger showing up at Mike Tomlin's weekly press conference wearing a suit and a pair of horn-rimmed glasses. He goes around and introduces himself as Kent Clark, the new reporter for the Harrisburg Patriot.

The Steelers beat writers and the TV reporters who are there shake his hand and welcome him to the beat and it never occurs to them that he's actually the Steelers quarterback.

A few minutes later, Kent Clark asks Mike Tomlin a question and Tomlin answers him without ever wondering why his quarterback is sitting among the filthy media wearing a suit and glasses.

Of course, since the news conference is televised live, thousands of people see this new guy asking a question, but not one of them calls a talk show and asks why Big Ben was asking questions at the press conference.

The Daily Planet needs an overhaul.

CHAPTER 35

THE BEST I EVER SAW

MARIO Lemieux has come a long way. He's not only the owner of the franchise that drafted him with the first overall pick in 1984, he *looks* like the quintessential team owner. Hell, he has the look of a distinguished United States senator.

Not bad for a kid who never finished high school.

I remember the first time I met him in June of 1984. He had just arrived in Pittsburgh for the first time and my brother Paul, who was working for the Penguins, had picked him up at the airport and given me the scoop on where he was staying.

I wasn't working that night but I called the assignment desk at WTAE-TV and told them to have a cameraman meet me downtown in the lobby of the Hyatt Hotel (now the Marriott). I brought my 12-year-old hockey-playing son Brett along with me and we met Lemieux in the Hyatt lobby. He was about three months away from his 19th birthday, skinny, very shy and spoke very little English. I didn't get much out of him but that didn't matter. What mattered was giving the people of Pittsburgh their first look at the kid who was going to save a franchise.

Who knew he would have to save it three times?

Mario Lemieux was a big deal at the time but only to the extent that a hockey player could be a big deal in Pittsburgh. Despite what the official attendance figures may have shown, in 1983-84, the Penguins averaged about 6,000 fans per game and very few games were televised. They were the fourth or fifth most important team in town behind the Steelers,

Pirates, Pitt football and probably Pitt basketball. There was nothing near the media frenzy that would happen in a similar situation in 2010.

A few months later, the Penguins opened their training camp at the Mt. Lebanon ice arena. They had been using the Mt. Lebanon facility for years as a practice rink during the season and on most days 10 fans would have been a big crowd. It became obvious right away that Lemieux had changed things. The Penguins opened their first scrimmage to the public and it was standing-room only with people being turned away at the door. Early in the scrimmage, Lemieux had the crowd roaring when he made a ridiculous pass to Rick Kehoe, who turned it into a goal.

It was one of those "all you had to see" moments. It became obvious in the first few minutes of the scrimmage that this skinny, 18-year-old kid was the best player on the ice and whoever was second wasn't even close.

I went back to WTAE and told the sports producer, Tim Kiely, that, right now, this kid may be the most exciting athlete in Pittsburgh. Tim told me to calm down, but he hadn't seen the kid play yet.

By the start of the season, everybody knew that Lemieux was something special and he really got a buzz going when he scored a goal on opening night in Boston on his first shift.

Hockey fans knew right away that this kid had "from another planet" qualities, but he was a hockey player and that meant that a huge portion of local sports fans would take a long time to realize how special he was.

I remember doing a commentary on KDKA-TV in 1986 telling people who hadn't taken the time to watch Lemiuex that they needed to start paying attention. I remember saying, "He's Babe Ruth. He's Jimmy Brown. We're talking about a guy who is going to be one of the all-time greats in his sport." I can also remember getting the feeling that some of the people on the set and in the newsroom thought I was getting carried away.

They were like so many other sports fans. They didn't understand or like hockey and the Penguins had never won anything. They weren't able to appreciate how special Lemieux was, that he wasn't just another good or even great young player, but a once-in-a-lifetime transformational super star.

Sometime in 1986 I wrote in my column that the greatest hockey player in the world was no longer living in Edmonton. I wrote that he was living in Pittsburgh. I took some heat for that, too. It wouldn't be the last time I was accused of going overboard in my assessment of Mario Lemiuex.

Pretty soon, things began to change in the newsroom. People who had never paid attention to hockey started tuning the monitors in their cubicles to Penguins' telecasts. Lemieux would turn a defender inside out and score a spectacular goal and you could hear shouts of disbelief coming from some of the people who had rolled their eyes when I had compared him to Babe Ruth.

By 1986 or 1987 Lemieux was the most exciting athlete in Pittsburgh and whoever was second (probably Louis Lipps of the Steelers) wasn't close.

Here's a statement that will still get some eyes rolling: Mario Lemieux is the best player in a team sport that I have ever seen. That's right.

Better than Joe Montana.

Better than Jimmy Brown.

Better than Walter Payton.

Better than Barry Bonds and, yeah, better than Michael Jordan.

I cannot imagine any player in any sport being better than Lemieux was in the 1988-89 season when he finished with 199 points. That was 16 points shy of the record set by Wayne Gretzky.

Gretzky wins the stats argument over Lemieux hands-down, but, in hockey, you get a point for an assist and to get an assist, the guy on the other end of your pass has to score a goal.

Everybody knows that Gretzky played with Hall of Famers when he set the record and Lemieux played on a line with Rob Brown, who, without Lemieux, was a marginal NHL player and Bob Errey, who was a very good, two-way player but never scored more than the 26 goals he had in that 1988-89 season playing on Lemieux's wing.

Michael Jordan was pretty good, too. I like to call him the Mario Lemieux of the NBA. Jordan played in a league that relaxed its rules on traveling and palming the ball to allow him to shine.

And sell tickets.

Lemieux played in a league that went out of its way not to enforce the rules on interference and holding that would have allowed him to shine.

And sell tickets.

And get a few more games on national TV.

I'm here to tell you that if Lemieux had played on that Oilers team with Jari Kuri, Glenn Anderson. Mark Messier and Paul Coffey, he would have scored at least 250 points.

I can't prove it. All I can do is tell you that I saw Lemieux play that season and I have never seen a player dominate games the way he did night-in and night-out. I really don't believe any player in major professional sports has ever been as dominant as Lemieux was in 1988-89.

And, again, he did it while having to fight through clutching and grabbing that was supposed to be illegal. He also had to deal with Neanderthal referees who thought that, because Lemieux was so big, it was only fair to let the smaller guys bend the rules to even things out.

You know, kind of like the way the NBA treated Wilt Chamberlin.

Lemieux scored a lot of spectacular, timely goals, but if I had to pick out one goal that I'll always remember, it came at the end of a season in which the Penguins didn't make the playoffs.

It was Saturday, April 2, 1988, in Washington. It was the second-to-last game of the season and the Penguins were in a situation where they had to win their last two games and get help from some other teams to make the playoffs.

Lemieux scored three goals and dominated the game as usual, but at the end of regulation the score was 6-6. The Penguins' coach, Pierre Creamer, mistakenly thought that they only had to tie the game to stay alive for the playoffs. The players knew otherwise.

I was sitting in the press box, which was at ice level, directly behind the goal being defended by the Capitals in overtime. Eddie Johnston, the Penguins general manager, was the only other person sitting there and he was right next to me. During the game I got great commentary from E.J., but the best comments didn't come from his mouth. They came from his elbows.

Every time Lemieux did something ridiculous, which was often, E.J. would just give me four or five quick jabs in the ribs. He knew the Penguins had to win and with less than a minute left in overtime, Lemieux picked up the puck in his own end and headed up the ice toward us. As he came across the blue line, two defensemen and goalie Pete Peeters were waiting for him. Somehow, Lemieux's skates (probably illegally) were cut out from under him. As he slid on his back toward the goal, he managed to get the blade of his stick under the puck and flip it up behind Peters and under the crossbar.

Game over. Penguins win 7-6.

E.J. gave me one last hard jab in the ribs, jumped up and said, "He's the best fuckin' player in the world" and headed for the locker room.

It was a spectacular goal but it was more than that. It was the culmination of one of the best examples I had ever seen of a player taking his team on his shoulders and not allowing it to lose. It was also the last minute of a game that they had to win in order to make the playoffs for the first time in five years. (As it turned out, despite also winning their last game, the Penguins fell short.)

I went to the locker room to do the post-game interviews and after I was finished I did something I had never done before and haven't done since. I went looking for Lemieux without a camera in tow and when I caught up to him walking out of the locker room, I stopped him, stuck out my hand and said, "I just want to tell you something. I have never seen anything that comes close to what you did out there today."

He gave me the Lemieux Nod and said, "Thanks."

CHAPTER 36

THE FIX WAS IN

MARIO Lemieux created a problem for me when he bought the Penguins and then had the nerve to call on the state and local politicians to follow through on their promises to build a new arena in Pittsburgh. I had been strongly opposed to tax dollars being spent on new facilities for the Pirates and Steelers, but I also knew that the Penguins couldn't stay in Pittsburgh without a new arena and I didn't want my grandkids to grow up without a hockey team. I couldn't care less about the Pirates moving out of town because, in my mind, they had moved out a long time ago and left a Triple "A" franchise behind and nobody thought the Steelers would move.

I got tired of hearing Penguins Chief Operating Officer Ken Sawyer whining about the lack of government support and Lemieux's whining was getting old, too, even if he did have a legitimate beef. I did think that the Penguins had one legitimate claim to make: It was wrong for the government to play favorites and give two of the three major professional sports franchises new stadiums and refuse the same for the Penguins. The politicians' argument was that the state/city/county couldn't afford it.

Lame argument.

They couldn't afford Heinz Field, PNC Park or, for that matter, Three Rivers Stadium and that didn't prevent them from shelling out the money.

The Penguins, Pirates and Steelers all seem to get along and root for each other but, make no mistake, they are in competition. There are only so many advertising and season ticket dollars to go around and don't think that the Penguins' recent success and their new arena hasn't hurt the Pirates financially. Lots of ticket buyers have bailed on the Pirates and spent their money on the Penguins. Same goes for luxury suite-renters and advertisers.

So, the state giving hundreds of millions to the Pirates and Steelers and not doing the same for the Penguins was the equivalent of, 25 years ago, the government giving millions of dollars to Kaufmann's and Horne's to build fancy new stores but telling Gimbel's there was no money left for them.

Then in 2003 I came across a story about the Calgary Flames asking the province of Alberta for permission to put slot machines in their new arena to generate revenue that would help them compete with the larger-market teams in Canada and the U.S.A. I didn't pay much attention to the details of the discussions between the Flames and Alberta officials. What jumped out at me was that the NHL was OK with the idea. Slots are legal in Alberta and the league had no problem with the Flames trying to get a piece of the gambling cash cow if it would make the franchise stronger.

In a column in the Pittsburgh-Tribune Review I suggested that the Penguins stop their whining about being given slot-machine revenue to build their new arena and go after the slots license itself and use the profits from the casino to fund their arena. I pointed out that the slots licenses were available for $50 million and that the Penguins could easily generate the $25 million a year to pay the mortgage on a new building and have millions and millions left over to reinvest in the team.

The column didn't generate any more response than usual and I didn't bring it up on TV or radio. I just kept the idea in the back of my mind and watched the usual singing and dancing that results when a sports team is begging for government money and the politicians are saying the government is broke.

In the meantime, I had been doing some research into the kind of money slot machines can generate and I was stunned. The slots licenses would truly be licenses to print money.

The media were full of reports about a group called Forrest Cities that was considered the frontrunner for the city of Pittsburgh's sole slots license. They were partnered with Harrah's, one of the biggest names in gambling, and they had lots of political connections. The Ratner family was involved and they had established a reputation for being experts at using political influence to get sweetheart development deals.

Their plan was to put the casino on the South Side.

Based on the history of Western Pennsylvania politics, it looked like the fix was in. Mayor Tom Murphy insinuated as much when he subtly told reporters, "The fix is in."

This was the mayor of Pittsburgh coming out in public and saying that the fix was in on a slots license that would make the owners of the casino hundreds of millions of dollars and journalists, who had lived in the region for years and years and had seen the rampant corruption and nepotism, did everything they could to quash any talk about anything being fixed.

Being the political junkie that I am, I was paying close attention to the process and I came across a story about a slots license in Illinois that became available and had been auctioned off. A company from Pennsylvania had been willing to bid $750 million. The city of Pittsburgh was in receivership, the state was floating in red ink and, instead of auctioning off the licenses for, say, $500 million, the idiot politicians were going to "award" them for $50 million?

Why?

Easy answer. If they're auctioned off, the politicians don't get to control who gets them and if they lose control they don't get to use the licenses and all the ancillary items surrounding them to hand out as political favors.

Here's the e-mail I sent to a Pennsylvania state senator:

"Senator _____

"In Cincinnati and Chicago (actually, Rosemont, Ill.) casino licenses are going for as much as $500 million. The one in Rosemont was awarded to a Pennsylvania company that was willing to invest $750 million. How can the state of Pa. actually be letting licenses go for as little as $50 million?"

I went on to point out that the purpose of the slots was to raise money for Pennsylvania and asked why the state was frittering away the chance to make hundreds of millions of dollars.

Then I wrote this to the state senator:

"Also, I'd be interested in what you think of my suggestion for the financing of a new arena. If the licenses are going to be awarded, why not award one to the Penguins? They get exclusive casino rights in Pittsburgh (for, say, 10 years?) in exchange for a new arena-financed totally by using a percentage of the $250 million gross to pay the $20 million debt service. Build it on the North Shore between PNC Park and Heinz Field. One estimate that I saw said that a slot machine in an urban, high-population area produced $550 per day in PROFIT (each slot at Mountaineer Resort produces $200 per day in profit). Do the math on what 1,000 slot machines located in an area where 2½ to 3 million people show up every year for sports events would produce. Imagine … a pro franchise paying for its own building. Mario would be a hero again."

I sent that email on Feb. 5, 2004. It only took three hours to get a response from the state senator who said he agreed with me that the licenses should be auctioned off and then went on to say:

"In regard to the Penguins idea — this is the first I've heard of it — it truly has potential and merit. I do believe this should be brought to the attention of the governor and others. I would like to forward your email to the governor."

In the meantime, I had been talking to my brother, Paul, about my idea and had given him some of the numbers that I had turned up showing the profitability of slot machines. He suggested I call his boss, Penguins COO Ken Sawyer, and run the idea by him. He set up a time for me to call Sawyer.

The conversation lasted less than five minutes. Like hundreds of thousands of other people in Western Pennsylvania, Sawyer didn't get it. He talked about the huge taxes that would have to be paid on slots earnings and wasn't able to focus on the fact that after paying 52 percent in taxes, the Penguins would still have hundreds of millions of dollars. He also didn't seem to grasp the concept of only needing $25 or $30 million a year from the slots to pay the mortgage on the new arena.

In Sawyer's defense, he had spent years trying to find ways to persuade the government to give the Penguins what they gave the Pirates and the Steelers and it's understandable that he would look at a wild idea like mine as a distraction.

Mario Lemieux was a different story.

My brother Paul told him what I had found out about slots and about my suggestion. Lemieux asked me to meet him at the Penguins Southpointe practice facility. I showed him the e-mail from the state senator, gave him some papers with all the information and he thanked me.

A few minutes later I sent this e-mail to the state senator:

"Senator _____ :
"I spoke with Mario Lemieux a few minutes ago and told him of your email to me regarding awarding the Penguins one of the casino licenses. He's very intrigued by the idea and says he plans to follow up on it."

The senator took about an hour and a half to respond:

"John:
"Excellent. We discussed your suggestion for state auctioning of license in caucus today. I also spoke with Senator _____ who is on the forefront of this issue and indicated I would provide him with your email to contact you."

When I informed the senator that I had been contacted by another senator from the opposing party, who said he thought it was a good idea and that I had been told by Lemieux that he planned to run the idea by Ken Sawyer, he emailed back:

"John:
"Why doesn't Mario talk to the governor —— he should meet with him!!! Your vision is right on target!!!!"

Five months later, on July 5, 2004, the Penguins announced that they would be pursuing a slots license and said that they would use the profits to fund a $250 million arena.

Now, you would think that, if your local government leaders were really interested in doing what's best for you and spending the money they confiscate from you wisely, they would pounce on the opportunity to save you $300 million.

Not in Pennsylvania.

I will always believe that the Penguins' decision to try to get a slots license was a major pain in the ass for Pittsburgh, Allegheny County and Pennsylvania politicians. The Forrest Cities group had all their political connections lined up and, until the Penguins' involvement, there was very little mention of any other group seriously pursuing the license.

A few days after the Penguins announced their attentions, Governor Ed Rendell was a guest on KDKA radio's evening talk show. When he was asked about the plan he all but dismissed it, laughed and said he couldn't see the NHL signing off on a plan that would allow one of its teams to be so closely associated with gambling.

Fast Eddie was either being dishonest or showing how out-of-touch he was. He either knew that the NHL had already signed off on a similar plan in Calgary and was misleading the listeners or he hadn't taken the time to actually call the NHL and find out.

I'm betting on the former.

Again, this was a plan that could save the taxpayers $300 million and the governor wouldn't give it the time of day.

Why? I think it was because the fix was in for Forrest Cities and the governor didn't want anyone to take the Penguins plan seriously.

If not for the Penguins' late entry into the process, very little attention would have been paid to who was going to get the license. Voters who knew how things work in Western Pennsylvania would have expected it go to somebody's brother-in-law or the otherwise well-connected.

The prospect of losing the Penguins changed everything and the sports talk shows were filled with callers demanding that the Penguins' plan to pursue a slots license be taken seriously.

Instead of the typical backroom deal, this was going to be a public process with a big, bright light shining on it.

Politician after politician, given the chance to at least enthusiastically endorse the idea of saving $300 million, went out of their way to express their neutrality or dismiss it.

The Penguins and their idea wouldn't go away and a few days before Christmas in 2005, they announced that they were partnering with Isle of

Capri Casinos and Nationwide Realty to apply for the slots license. They pledged $290 million in upfront money for the new arena and unveiled plans for a $1 billion development plan for the 28 acres surrounding Mellon Arena.

By this time, there were a lot of elected officials getting behind the Penguins, but the most important players, Rendell and Allegheny County Executive Dan Onorato, were still doing their best not to show any enthusiasm for the plan. Onorato said it wouldn't be fair to the other applicants if he supported any one group.

That, of course, was a huge, steaming pile of horse manure.

Who ended up with the license and where the casino would be built were huge issues that could affect the financial health of the region for the next 50 years. A government "leader" would have taken the time to investigate all three proposals (a third applicant, Detroit native Don Barden, who owned several casinos, had announced his intentions the day after the Penguins announced their partnership with Isle of Capri) and thrown his support behind the one that he thought would be best for his constituents.

When several city, county and state politicians called a press conference to announce their support for the Penguins' bid, Onorato, according to my source in the state senate, let many of them know how disappointed he was.

When I reported that on the air, Onorato called the KDKA-TV news director and complained. He denied being upset with the people who supported the Penguins' plan and denied that he had called the Penguins' supporters and scolded them.

My source stood by his story.

The longer the ugly process went on, the more obvious it became that, as you would expect in Western Pennsylvania, corruption was everywhere.

One former, high-level Democratic operative told me that, in all his years in politics, he had never seen so much corruption and he was referring mostly to Democrats.

My favorite was the awarding of slot-machine distribution licenses. Instead of allowing the new casinos to just go out and buy slot machines, the slime balls in Harrisburg decided to make the casinos buy their machines through a state-licensed distributor. This, of course, created some high-paying, unnecessary jobs that could be handed out as political favors. There were regulations in place to prevent Pennsylvania elected or appointed officials from being eligible for these licenses to print money. But when the wife of the Turnpike Commissioner and the toddler son of a former state rep turned lobbyist — who had donated over $100,000 to Rendell — showed up as applicants, the plan for slot machine distributors was eventually scrapped, despite Rendell's best efforts.

As the process dragged on, the local sports media were mostly behind Lemieux's plan, but Pittsburgh Post-Gazette columnist Bob Smizik criticized the local talk-show hosts who spent large portions of their shows campaigning for Lemieux's plan and started referring to them as "MFOM" — Media Friends of Mario. I respect Smizik as much as any columnist I've ever read and I think I agree with him most of the time, but I don't remember him referring to the media cheerleaders for the baseball and football stadiums as "Media Friends of the Rooneys" or "Media Friends of McClatchy." I thought the inconsistency was glaring and amazingly unfair.

Of course, as it turned out, the Pennsylvania Gaming Board passed over the Penguins and picked the worst applicant of the three, Don Barden. Of the seven applicants for Pennsylvania slots licenses, Barden was the only minority. On the day that it was announced that Barden had been awarded the license, his spokesman said on the radio that he was sure Barden's minority status played a role in the board's decision.

I will always believe that the light being shined on the process because of the Penguins pursuit of a slots license prevented the local politicians from giving it to their friends from Forrest Cities.

About a half an hour after Barden acquired the license, it became obvious that he was in over his head. He eventually had to be bailed out by another buyer and, at this writing, the casino on the North Shore is underperforming.

In the final analysis, the Penguins applying for the slots license ended up being the right way to go. Because of the pressure created by the prospect of Pittsburgh losing the Penguins, the other two applicants were forced to set aside a portion of their casino profits to fund the Consol Energy Center, where the Penguins will begin playing in October of 2010.

The building will keep the Penguins in town for at least another 30 years and it will also forever stand as a testament to local government corruption and stupidity.

The Penguins have a brand new $300 million arena and I'm satisfied in the knowledge that the plan that most likely made the difference in keeping NHL hockey in Pittsburgh began with me.

Although, Steigerwald Arena Presented By Consol Energy does have a nice ring to it.

And I wouldn't turn my nose up at a couple of lifetime season tickets.

Or maybe a hat.

Mario knows where I can be reached.

CHAPTER 37

THE 6
(morning, noon, 4, 5, 10 and 11)
O'CLOCK SNEWS.

WHEN I went on the air at Channel 4 for the first time on December 18, 1978, Pittsburgh was either the 10th or 11th largest TV market in the United States. Pittsburgh and Cleveland had been going through a period of fluctuating between 10th and 11th.

The last I checked, Pittsburgh was down to 23rd.

You can thank all of those people waving Terrible Towels at Steelers games in Phoenix, Miami, Charlotte and every other NFL city for that.

I replaced a guy named Steve Zabriskie, who had been doing a lot of work for ABC on weekends and would go on to work there full time.

That's where people who worked on TV in Pittsburgh usually went. If it wasn't the network, it was the network-owned station in one of the Big Three markets, New York, Los Angeles or Chicago.

Sam Nover, who had been working for WIIC (now WPXI) had been getting some work at NBC and would eventually be hired full time there. Dick Stockton, who was a star at CBS at the time, had worked at KDKA in the late '60s and early '70s and is still doing NFL games for Fox.

Pittsburgh was the Big Time for anybody working in local news around the country. When the local network affiliates here were looking to hire new people, they solicited tapes from all over the country and usually hired reporters and/or anchors who were working in the top 15-50 markets.

I remember in 1980, after Channel 4 had made the decision to expand their 6 o'clock news to an hour, being in News Director Joe Rovitto's office amid a sea of tapes that had been submitted for one of the weekend anchor positions.

I'm not exaggerating when I say that his small office was thigh-high in ¾-inch video tapes.

One of those tapes had been sent by a nice looking young woman named Sally Wiggin, who was also in the office at the time for an interview.

Sally was a smart woman who had studied Chinese at the University of Michigan and was working in Birmingham, Alabama. As anybody who's been living in Pittsburgh the last 30 years knows, Wiggin got the job.

Thirty years later and she's still there.

Pretty good hire.

The difference between then and now is that, now, when the Pittsburgh stations hire new reporters and anchors, they're getting them from Clarksburg, West Virginia. They're coming from markets 50-100. Huntsville instead of Birmingham. Youngstown instead of Cincinnati.

And that's a long way from being the only difference.

When I started at Channel 4, Paul Long and Don Cannon were the anchors. Cannon had been there about 10 years since coming from a UHF station in Chicago. Long was a newsman who had worked as a writer and a radio reporter for years before getting into TV and had left KDKA to join WTAE the same year that Cannon was hired, 1969. Cannon had a background in radio. They both were *newsmen*.

They liked the idea of being on television, but their motivation for getting into the business was a love of covering the news.

Too many — probably most — of the people getting into local news the last 10 or 15 years, were/are motivated by a strong desire to be on TV.

Or worse, to be a celebrity.

Bill Burns of KDKA didn't get into TV because he wanted to be a celebrity. He was a *newsman*.

Same with Adam Lynch at WIIC (WPXI).

Another pretty important difference was that the stations actually covered news. There was no CNN or Fox News Channel. Reporters had to be conversant in national and world affairs. Today, an anchor has to be able to read a Teleprompter and a reporter has to be pretty good at chasing ambulances and fire trucks.

I'll let you in on a little secret.

A few years ago, as the November sweeps were about to begin, the general manager of KDKA was giving the usual pre-sweeps pep talk to the newsroom staff, including anchors, reporters and producers. He told them that the two most important areas to focus on were weather and the Steelers, in that order. He said those were the topics that drove the ratings.

You can be sure that the general managers and news directors at the other two local news operations felt the same way and let their staffs know.

I don't know about you, but I can get a 10-day weather forecast on my phone in 30 seconds or less. Why do I need to tune into a newscast and then sit through 4 minutes of cold fronts and high-pressure systems and the meteorologist showing me all of his or her bells and whistles?

Check out any local station in the country and you will see that they are doing the weather exactly the way they did it in 1985, only with trickier technology and prettier pictures.

They've all been told by consultants that viewers' Number One reason for tuning in is to get a weather forecast. Somebody has needed to tell them for a long time that that doesn't mean that the viewers want to sit through four minutes of meteorological gobbledygook before they get it.

Especially now, when they can get it on their cell phone with the push of a key.

The weathermen and women are always feeling pressure from the newsroom to make the forecast as dire as possible and if there's an inch of snow on the ground, it's the lead story on all three stations.

Trust me.

The anchors and reporters you're watching, on those days when an inch of snow is turned into "The Blizzard of '77," are embarrassed. They're just reading what the producer put in the Teleprompter.

If you're looking for creativity and originality, you're not going to find it in your local TV newsroom.

And it's not just Pittsburgh.

If you were to put 300 televisions on one huge wall and tune them into the ABC, CBS and NBC affiliates in each of the top 100 markets in the Eastern Time Zone, at 6:14 p.m. all 300 sets on the wall would be showing a local weather forecast.

At 6:25, every one would be doing local sports.

I'm not exaggerating. Every single one of those TV stations would be doing the same thing. They all do the same thing every day and it's basically the same thing they've been doing since 1962.

That's why local TV news is on it's way to becoming irrelevant. Like newspapers.

I'll let you in on another dirty little secret. The longer the people you're watching on your favorite newscast have been around, the more embarrassed they are by what's happened to their profession. The people who have been at it for 20 years or more were working in local news when it was defensible. They're aware of what it once was and what it has become.

It still pays well. That's why they're still hanging around.

At KDKA it was (and probably still is) mandatory for female anchors to wear black and gold for newscasts that featured extensive Steelers playoff coverage. A little sexist, don't you think, considering that the men were never required to do the same?

How can any self-respecting news anchor not be embarrassed when he or she has to lead a newscast with the earthshaking news that Ben (not Ben Roethlisberger — just Ben) has returned from his vacation in Switzerland? In the summer of 2006, all three stations chased and harassed him at the Pittsburgh airport.

Then, a few months after Roethlisberger recovered from injuries resulting from riding his motorcycle without a helmet, KDKA had videotape of Roethlisberger riding helmetless on the streets of Pittsburgh.

Based on the coverage that his accident received, that deserved to be the lead story on the newscast. The news director destroyed the tape and later denied to Sports Illustrated that he had ever seen it.

In that case, "Ben" wasn't big news because showing the tape might have pissed off the Steelers.

After Roethlisberger was accused of sexual assault by a woman in a Milledgeville, Georgia, bar in March of 2010, there were more stories about the stations being less than enthusiastic about covering too many angles of the story.

Again — in deference to the Steelers.

I know of one sports reporter who caused a major panic in his station's newsroom by saying out loud that Troy Polamalu had cut his hair. He made the story up just to prove to himself that there was no sanity left in the newsroom. The female producer was apoplectic.

I'm here to tell you that, if the story had been true, it would have been the lead story on all three local newscasts.

And I'm not kidding.

There's not a better TV reporter in the country than John Shumway. I don't know of anyone who is better at doing live, on-the-scene reports and I've told him many times that he should be working for one of the networks, but, for years, KDKA wasted his talent by assigning him to the Steelers beat.

He would do his usual good job of reporting but his presence at Bill Cowher's press conferences was an embarrassment to him and the entire news operation.

His talents were wasted.

Good female anchors and reporters have embarrassed themselves and will continue to embarrass themselves by doing fawning interviews with Steelers and, more recently, Penguins, that are only done in November, February or May — the three big sweeps months.

There's such a lack of enterprise, originality, creativity and good news-sense that the best the news directors and their producers can come up with to boost their ratings is one more sit-down with "Ben" or "Troy" or "Hines" and maybe "Sid."

It's enough to make any self-respecting "journalist" puke.

The sports producers at all three stations start getting the e-mails from their bosses two or three weeks before the beginning of the sweeps month: "Can we get Ben?" "I want a sit down with Troy."

Management doesn't care that none of these people has anything to say that is worth repeating. If they can get "Ben" or "Troy" to sit down and read out of the phone book, they'll take it. Why? Because they can promote it. If they can sucker you into watching and you have one of those meters on your TV, it doesn't matter what "Ben" or "Troy" says or doesn't say. You made the meter click and that's all that matters.

The city of Pittsburgh is in receivership and the state government reeks of corruption. It would be nice — and the viewers would be a lot better served — if all three stations spent as much time exposing that as they do trying to cover "Ben" and "Troy."

Or talking about an inch of snow.

Keep in mind what the KDKA GM said: The top two priorities are weather and the Steelers.

Ask your favorite 25-year-old if he or she ever watches the local news. You'll find he or she watches the news about as often as he or she reads the local newspaper — which is almost never. The Pittsburgh market has enough old people to allow KDKA, WPXI and WTAE to keep getting away with doing the news the same way they did it in 1975 for a while, but, as the old people die off, the local newscasts will begin to disappear.

I stopped watching local news several years ago. The only time I would see it was when I was on it or if I was in the sports office and/or newsroom and was exposed to it on a monitor.

Time for another secret.

Lots of my friends, who are still reading and reporting the news, also stopped watching it a long time ago.

They're embarrassed by it and it's way too boring.

KDKA does three hours of news every day from 4 o'clock until 7. The other two stations each do 90 minutes from 5 until 6:30.

That's six hours of evening news every day. Do you know how many of those 360 minutes are devoted to commentary?

Zero.

Even the sports guys have stopped doing commentary.

There was a time when Bill Curry at KDKA and Myron Cope at WTAE were doing daily commentaries and Sam Nover at WPXI would do them when the mood struck, which was fairly often.

I did regular commentaries for a while at the request of the news director and Stan Savran was more than willing to take his shots from time to time.

I also was happy to break the rules of journalism from time to time and mix an opinion in with my reporting. I took a good bit of criticism for it but I noticed that my paychecks kept getting bigger and decided to keep doing it.

I also always took the approach that it was "only" sports and expressing an opinion on who should be starting at quarterback for the Steelers was quite a bit different from coming out in favor of a presidential candidate.

One doesn't matter, the other does.

Al Julius had a full-time job for 15 years doing nothing but commentaries on KDKA's 6 o'clock news.

You know why nobody's doing it anymore?

Simple.

Somebody might be offended.

Remember, we're talking about 2010 here. Everybody has an opinion on everything and everybody has the ability through blogs and Twitter and a thousand other online vehicles to make those opinions available to every person on the planet.

But, sorry, no opinions on the city being bankrupt or the state house being run by people who make organized crime look like the Knights of Columbus.

(Sorry. Those softball "editorials" by the station manager don't count.)

No opinions on how local politicians should vote on the various life-changing pieces of legislation that are proposed every day.

Government officials say they're not available and they're left alone. Steelers, who have no obligation to speak to the public, are harassed at the airport and asked what kind of cheese they brought back with them from their vacation, but when they do deserve to be questioned for being in the news for the wrong reasons, they're let off the hook because of a fear of losing access.

When was the last time you saw a local public official ambushed in a parking lot by a reporter with a camera?

A few years ago, the KDKA news department was having a hard time getting former Pittsburgh mayor Tom Murphy to submit to an interview. Here's what I suggested to the news director:

Put an empty chair on the news set with Tom Murphy's name on it. Every night at 6 o'clock, take a shot of the empty chair and have the anchor say, "We've been trying to get the mayor to comment on this story but he has not made himself available. We think this is an important issue and our viewers deserve an explanation. We are keeping this seat empty with the mayor's name on it and he has an open invitation to come in for a live interview. We will continue to show you the empty chair until the mayor shows a willingness to come in and fill it."

I would show the chair at least once a night and I would have the anchors remind the viewers that their mayor is still hiding from them. If I knew that a station was willing to take that approach, I might actually feel compelled to tune in once in a while.

The news director was amused by the idea and actually said he thought it would make for good TV, but he and I both knew it would never happen.

Too original. Too offensive.

The time would be better spent adding one more minute-and-a-half weather update.

Your local TV stations actually think that you will be offended or bored or both if they hold your local "leaders'" feet to the fire. If they're right, then they have succeeded in dumbing-down their audience to World Wrestling Federation levels.

A TV news operation that is doing its job should be feared and despised by most of the people in local government. The station would have at least one reporter who would harass elected officials until they were willing to face tough questions.

Local news is all about murders, fires and traffic accidents. Do your eyes glaze over when you hear your favorite anchor start to voice-over video from the overnight fire in Etna? The one in which nobody was hurt and no arson is suspected?

How about the fatal traffic accident three counties away? Of course, you feel bad when you hear that someone is killed, but is your life enriched by the knowledge?

Do you have any idea how many resources are needed to get you those pictures of the fire that you don't care about? An assignment editor has to monitor the police radio or take the phone call. A cameraperson has to be sent out in a news car to get the pictures. In some cases a reporter would be sent, too. The video is brought back to the station and given to someone to edit a 30-second clip for the newscast.

All this for something that no one, other than the people directly involved in the fire/murder/accident, cares about.

I have a little extra time to kill here, so I'm going to give local news directors everywhere a way to set themselves apart from their competitors and actually get better ratings.

Watch Fox News.

Wait. Before you watch, check the cable ratings.

Fox wins everything and it's not close. They get more viewers than CNN and MSNBC combined.

Why? For starters, Fox isn't liberal. That sets it apart from every other network. But what makes Fox so much more compelling is debate.

And confrontation.

And controversy.

Of course, confrontation and controversy follow from debate. I know it's national news and that's a different animal, but if a Pittsburgh station were to hire a local version of Bill O'Reilly and do a local newscast that was produced in segments the way that "The O'Reilly Factor" is produced, it just might save local news.

No more weather at 15 after the hour unless the weather actually is a story because it might actually have an effect on the viewers' day. No sports unless it's either a really big story or includes some controversy or both.

Politicians would be put on notice that they would be invited in to answer the tough questions put to them by the local O'Reilly and, if they didn't come in, they could expect to be ambushed by a reporter and a camera at any time.

No voiceovers of traffic accidents or fires.

Murders don't make the news unless they have a major impact on the community. Actually, if a news director felt he had to devote some time to the typical local news trivia, it could all be done in a minute or two of voiceover before the first commercial break. Instead of devoting time and resources to finding people to chase ambulances and fire trucks, stations should hire good, smart, aggressive, creative producers who would be looking for compelling news stories that lend themselves to controversy and debate.

In the beginning, the ratings wouldn't come close to what the three stations are getting now, but it would be a lot less expensive to produce and that could translate to the corporate owners' favorite word.

Profit.

I used to sit in the sports office at KDKA and watch boring story after boring story come across the screen and wonder how we had any viewers left. It wasn't the reporters' fault. It was the story selection or the way a story was treated. I would constantly see stories that could be turned into compelling 15-minute segments if there had been anybody in management with the creativity or, more important, the guts to do it.

An example: There was a story, I believe in Westmoreland County, about a kid who showed up at school wearing a baseball cap with the Confederate flag on the front. I don't remember all the details, but I think he was sent home and the parents protested. I don't remember how it turned out, but the point is that the story got about a minute and a half of airtime and just kind of floated along with the rest of the flotsam in the newscast.

Here's what I would have done with the story:

I would have called the kid and his parents and invited them to come to the studio and offered them a limo if necessary. I also would have invited officials from the school and we would have had a nice debate about how offensive the Confederate flag is and whether the kid had the right to wear it to school.

If the school officials refused to come in, their names would be on empty chairs next to the kid and his parents.

I would have invited viewers to e-mail their comments and read some of them at the end of the newscast.

You can bring in all the high-paid consultants you want, but nobody is going to convince me that stories like that, done well, wouldn't bring you more viewers in the long run than a four-minute weather forecast or four minutes of fire/crash/murder video.

A show like this would require a strong personality, someone as obnoxious and aggressive as Bill O'Reilly and that would create a problem for local news stations because they stopped promoting personalities a long time ago,

There was a time when stations liked to promote personalities. KDKA knew that Bill Burns *was* KDKA and they liked it. WTAE promoted Don Cannon, Paul Long and meteorologist Joe DiNardo as a team. They produced promos that highlighted what regular guys they were and how well they got along. Then somebody got tired of paying big money for personalities and decided that it was call letters that got people to watch, not the personalities.

They were wrong, of course, but they saved a lot of money. They also now have newscasts that consist of newsreaders who have become indistinguishable and interchangeable and only serve as vessels for the writings of 25-year-old producers, many of whom would have a tough time naming Pennsylvania's two senators.

Secret time again.

It makes no difference who's reading the news to you. The anchors you see are just reading scripts that have been handed to them by a producer several minutes before the newscast.

Any competent anchor on any Pittsburgh station, or any station in the country for that matter, could stroll into any one of the three stations at 5:30 or 5:45 and anchor the 6 o'clock news and you wouldn't notice the difference.

One anchor could get up out of his chair in mid-sentence and allow another anchor to finish the sentence as he's taking his seat and it would be a seamless transition.

There is no personality wanted or allowed.

The people you see aren't talking to you. They're reading somebody else's words to you.

In the mid-90s, the Neilsen company switched to a new ratings system. They went from written diaries to meters that are attached to the viewer's TV. In the Pittsburgh market there are approximately 1,000 viewers who are monitored. If three KDKA viewers have diarrhea on a given night and don't get off the toilet in time to tune into the newscast, WTAE will probably win the ratings for that newscast by a tenth of a point.

A news producer now is all about managing the clock so that the newscast registers on the meters of as many viewers as possible. That has become much more important than content. It's about positioning a story so that a viewer watches long enough to register on the meter in more than one segment

It's all very boring. Just like most newscasts.

To give you one last idea of how things have changed, I'll take you back to December of 1978 again. It was my first sportscast for WTAE. A 23-year-old desk assistant (news writer) named Bob Reichblum was assigned to help me with the formatting of the show. There was a system that had to be followed in order to communicate with the director in the booth and he was there to make sure I got it right.

Reichblum, not too long after that, became the executive producer of "Good Morning America." The news anchor that night was Mike Schneider. He went on to become the news anchor on both the "Today" show and "Good Morning America" and worked as a fill-in for Peter Jennings on ABC's "World News Tonight."

When Schneider left, he was replaced by Faith Daniels, who also went on to network jobs at NBC and CBS and filled in for Dan Rather on CBS.

Most of the people who are doing Reichblum's job in newsrooms now are underpaid, overworked clerks who, after a few years of writing voiceovers for fires/murders/traffic accidents, move on to something better and it usually has nothing to do with television.

You can be pretty sure there are no network stars toiling in Pittsburgh's local newsrooms today. Not necessarily because they're not as talented or not as smart, but, because they've been trained to talk an audience that considers "The Price is Right" compelling television.

CHAPTER 38

LISTS

SOME lists listed in no particular order of importance:

BEST POSTGAME INTERVIEW

TERRY BRADSHAW

No contest here. I knew in 1980 that he would be a TV star when his career ended. I can only remember one time when he refused to talk to the media after a game. I can't remember which game it was but he politely asked if we would mind if he passed on the post-game interviews. Nobody in the media even thought about complaining or criticizing him because we had all seen him stand and answer every question after every win and, more important, after every loss. A real standup guy, oozing personality and charisma, he was a can't-miss for TV. He liked to mess with the media and say one thing to one reporter and the opposite to another but that just added to the fun.

BUBBY BRISTER

Another stand up guy who loved the stage and wasn't shy about giving it right back to the media. I always liked his feistiness and I also think he was another casualty of Bill Cowher's total ineptitude when it came to evaluating and developing quarterbacks. I still think he was a better quarterback than Neil O'Donnell — O'Donnell's Super Bowl appearance notwithstanding.

JIM LEYLAND

Anybody who cries at the drop of a hat is a TV guy's dream. Leyland didn't just wear his emotions on his sleeve, he wore them on his chest, shoulders and lower body. He was pretty bad when he took over as Pirates manager in 1985 and actually looked like he was going to be deadly. But he learned to like the daily battle with the media and understood better than most that the guys sitting in front of him after every game waiting to second-guess him were just doing their jobs.

KEVIN STEVENS

Once again, a stand-up guy. Are you noticing a trend here? He was the guy in the Penguins' locker room to whom you could go knowing that he would show the same patience for your questions whether it was a 6-1 loss or a 6-1 win. Nobody was all that surprised when he predicted four straight wins after the Penguins went down two games to none to the Bruins in the 1991 playoffs.

JOE GREENE

He was as intimidating as they come but also the rock of the Steelers' locker room. If you wanted the last word on what the game just completed meant, you went to Joe. He didn't suffer fools well and even way back then the media horde was full of them. I'll never forget the poor slob who kept shoving his microphone too close to Greene's face during a postgame media scrum in front of his locker. Greene wasn't in a very good mood, so it was probably after a loss. Joe kept pushing the mic away from his face and finally on the third or fourth time, without looking away from the person he was responding to, he just grabbed the plastic mic in his huge hand and crushed it while continuing to answer the question.

JACK LAMBERT

He had very little patience with the media but, unlike too many others, he understood that they had a job to do and his grouchiness consistently produced good sound bites. It really wasn't a good idea to approach him after a loss until after he smoked a couple of cigarettes, which he used to do while still in full uniform, sitting against the wall in the training room.

BOB BERRY

He was the coach of some really bad Penguins teams in the early '80s and was happy to tell you in great detail after every loss just how bad the team was. One of his favorite expressions was "We were flatter than piss on a plate." He also was known to refer to his players as "two-bit circus performers."

LEE FLOWERS

He was a nasty player on the field who delivered some vicious hits from his strong safety position and he was a loose cannon who was never shy about spewing good bulletin-board material for the Steelers' opponents. As is often the case with the volatile ones, he was especially good after losses.

WORST POSTGAME INTERVIEW

MARIO LEMIEUX

I'm guessing that he would be proud to at the top of anybody's worst interview list because it was obvious that he worked at being bad in the hopes that people would leave him alone. Lemieux just didn't like talking to the media. He didn't have a perfect record of showing up for the postgame interviews but with guys like him who are relentlessly hounded by the media, he was good enough and he was always polite and respectful. He was a master at saying nothing until he decided it was time to use his clout to send a message. You may remember the uproar in the mid-'90s when he decided to refer to the NHL as "a garage league."

NEIL O'DONNELL

Another master of the art of saying nothing. The Steelers quarterback's comments are as important if not more important to the media than the head coach's after a game. I don't remember ever hearing O'Donnell say anything worth repeating, but, there I was, game after game, sticking my mic in his face. There was always the fear that he might actually say something interesting or inflammatory and you would miss it.

TROY POLAMALU

This guy makes Lemiuex sound like Chad Ochocinco. You couldn't ask for a nicer or more humble guy, but talk about a deadly postgame interview. He could intercept three passes in a game and run two of them back for touchdowns and all you would get out of him is that he is "blessed."

JAMIE DIXON

Another nice, polite, unassuming guy who coaches a lot better than he talks. He has improved over the years and is much better now than he was when he first took over as head basketball coach at Pitt, but he still looks amazingly uncomfortable and after his press conferences almost always leaves you wishing for less.

CAREER-ENDING INJURY LIST

This one needs some explaining. Over the course of my career I kept a running mental list of guys who would be doing their sports a favor if they sustained a career-ending injury. I guess I could have called it a "Wish They Would Retire List," but these guys were never going to walk away from the money they were making. When I put a guy on my list, which I never made public and only discussed with people I trusted, it was with the understanding that I wasn't wishing any serious permanent injury on anybody. I just was hoping for an injury that would end the guy's career and send him off to a happy, healthy, wealthy, pain-free rest of his life. Very few players made this list and you really had to be a bad guy to show up on it. I never had more than three or four on it at a given time. I don't have any current players on the list, but here are the last four to make it.

GREG LLOYD

Boy, was this guy a piece of work. This is a guy who insisted on parking in the handicapped space in front of the Steelers offices at Three

Rivers Stadium. Just a bad guy all the way around. Once, after a loss, as I was trying to get my microphone in front of Rod Woodson, whose locker was next to Lloyd's, I was forced to partially block Lloyd from getting to his locker. Lloyd gave me a shove. Not a nudge, a shove and said, "Get the fuck outta the way." I said, "How about excuse me?" Lloyd grabbed the towel hanging in front of his crotch and said, "Excuse these nuts." That was bad, but that alone would never be enough to get a guy on my "Career-Ending Injury List." He made it because of what I saw him do to other reporters and because of some of the stories I heard about his off-the-field encounters with fans, security guards, etc. I can honestly tell you that there were a lot of happy reporters in the Gator Bowl press box in Jacksonville that day in 1996 when he blew out an ankle. The difference between them and me is that I was willing to admit (not on the air, of course) that I was glad when I heard he wouldn't be around for the rest of the year.

TOM BARRASSO

This is one miserable human being. At least he was when there were reporters around. I can't point to a single incident, but this was a guy who I thought would make the NHL and Pittsburgh better by disappearing. He was a great goalie and deserves to be in the Hall of Fame but, apparently because of a bad experience or two with reporters he thought had treated him unfairly, he treated everybody in the media the same. Like dogs. I have no patience for that kind of stupidity and wanted him to be gone.

BARRY BONDS

Come on. You don't really need me to explain this one, do you?

MICHAEL VICK

I'm a certified dog trainer and the owner of two Golden Retrievers. Enough said? This is one case where I might waive the happy, healthy, pain-free clause.

FAVORITE ROAD VENUES

Keep in mind that I was lucky enough to see these places both from great vantage points in the press box and from down on the field (or ice).

1 — CLEVELAND MUNICIPAL STADIUM

By far, my favorite place to watch a football game. It was almost 40 years old the first time I saw a game there in 1970 and was already a dump. It was really ugly by the time the Browns played their last game there in 1995. I always hoped that the Steelers played in Cleveland late in the season, preferably in December. The colder and uglier the weather, the better. Lake Erie was right next door and that produced some great football weather and, of the 83,000 who showed up for every game, at least 82,500 were drunk. The Dawg Pound showed up for the last 10 or 15 years and they were a perfect fit. They also were spontaneously spawned. They weren't created by an ad agency or a TV station. For some reason, guys just started showing up in dog masks. Some came in full costume. If the game was played late in the season, you could count on the field being in terrible shape. Clumps of grass and lots of mud. Combine all that with the fact that the two teams always hated each other and the fans of the two teams hated each other even more and you had the perfect formula for a real football game.

It's something they'll never understand in San Diego or Miami.

Real football fans should always give the Browns and Cleveland credit for not building a domed stadium. It could have been easily justified. Unlike the two domed football stadiums built in Indianapolis, which I'll never understand.

2 — HOUSTON ASTRODOME

I don't normally like domed stadiums. In fact, as a general rule, I despise them, but I used to love watching the Steelers play the Houston Oilers in the Astrodome. The stadium had no atmosphere or character whatsoever, but the fans more than made up for it. In the late '70s and early '80s the Steelers played some huge games against the Oilers. The fans were right on top of the players and the noise in the Astrodome could cure dandruff. I've never seen a team have to play in a more hostile environment. They had a guy named "Crazy George" roaming the stadium and the place would go nuts when he started banging on his snare drum. The field was as hard as cement and both teams had hard-hitting defenses that made you wonder how everybody got out alive. I loved games in the Astrodome but hated Houston. It was my least favorite NFL city. I've been to the Texans' stadium and I wasn't impressed.

3 — LAMBEAU FIELD

Picture Heinz Field sitting in Cranberry Township or Upper St. Clair and you'll get an idea of what it looks like around Lambeau Field in Green Bay. The stadium just sits there in what looks like a suburb of an NFL city, a long punt away from a residential neighborhood. Of course, that's not what makes Lambeau Field special. It's the history. I think Notre Dame Stadium is the only other football venue that can call up the echoes the way the Packers' home field can. Real football fans everywhere should be glad that Lambeau hasn't been replaced by a dome. The last time I was there, the game was played in the snow. It doesn't get much better than that.

4 — BOSTON GARDEN

Talk about a beautiful dump. It looked and felt like it was built entirely out of wood and it smelled like hockey. The seats were jammed together and the upper decks seemed to actually hang out over the ice. I never saw a basketball game there, but seeing all of those Celtics championship banners hanging from the ceiling gave me chills. The fans could give you chills, too, for other reasons. I can remember, during the 1991 playoffs, leaving my seat in the press box to go back to the press lounge between periods and being shocked by the people I saw coming down from the upper level seats. They're still the dirtiest, toughest looking fans I've ever seen.

5 — ARROWHEAD STADIUM

I doubt that you'll find a lot of people in the Pittsburgh media who looked forward to trips to Kansas City, but I always did. I loved games at Arrowhead Stadium. Especially night games late in the season. Arrowhead had the same feel that Municipal Stadium in Cleveland had without the lake: Loud with real fans. Arrowhead seats over 70,000 and even the people in the upper deck look close to the field. I also like Kansas City. It reminds me of Pittsburgh.

BEST ASSIGNMENTS

I — PENGUINS STANLEY CUP RUNS, 1991 AND 1992

I never worked harder than I worked covering the Penguins' first two Stanley Cup winners and never enjoyed an assignment more. From early April until early June I didn't get a day off and just about every day was at least a 13-hour workday. Show up for practice at 10 in the morning and anchor the 11 p.m. sports. Go to the morning skate the next day at around 10, cover the game that night, do a live report on the 11 p.m. news. Practice the next morning. That was every day for about six weeks. We traveled to road games and some days we would catch an early flight the morning after a game and go directly to another practice after landing in Pittsburgh. I never got tired of it. Back then, there was a game almost every other night as opposed to recently when teams can go three or four days without a game. By having to follow the team on the road, I got a real appreciation for just how hard it is to win the Stanley Cup. It's the toughest championship in pro sports. I pointed that out often during my TV reports and after the playoffs ended in 1991, I was confronted by Andy Van Slyke in the Pirates locker room. He said, "I have a bone to pick with you. How can you say that the NHL championship is harder to win than a World Series? The Penguins finished third in their division and were still able to play for the championship. In baseball, you have to either win your division or qualify for one wild card spot."

(This exchange with Van Slyke would never happen now because local players never watch the local news.)

I had to explain to him that in the NHL there were also division winners who had to win three series just to get to the finals. I also pointed out that playing a hockey game every other night for six weeks is a little tougher on the body than playing seven baseball games in 10 days.

2 — 1979 WORLD SERIES

I never thought covering a World Series winner could finish second to covering a Stanley Cup winner and it only does because of the number of games. The Pirates played two series in 1979 to win their championship; the Penguins played four. For me it was always about the games. That's why, before Major League Baseball was ruined forever, I always liked baseball better than football.

More games.

The 1979 team will be forever associated with Sister Sledge's song "We Are Family" and it had a reputation as a fun-loving bunch, but they weren't all that much fun to cover. You couldn't ask for a more cooperative and friendly guy than the manager, Chuck Tanner, but there were some tough guys to deal with on that team, specifically, John Candelaria, Bert Blylven, Bill Madlock and John Milner. But it was an enjoyable team to watch. They were given no chance to beat the Orioles and they looked like they were going to prove everybody right when they went down three games to one.

During the season, the music was so loud in the locker room after games that even the writers had trouble hearing the players' answers. It was impossible to do TV or radio interviews. Late in the season, the local baseball writers went to General Manager Pete Peterson and said that unless something was done about the loud music they would boycott the locker room. Pete was a great guy, who was always friendly and accessible to the media and understood that they had a job to do. So he told the players that, from now on, they could not play music in the locker room for the first 10 minutes after a game.

Milner, who was one of the most miserable human beings ever to play a sport in Pittsburgh, parked himself in front of the music system controls. While he smoked a cigarette, he looked up at the clock and was nice enough to keep track of how much time was left before it would be impossible to do any more interviews.

He screamed out:

"Nine minutes, motherfuckers."
"Eight minutes, motherfuckers."

He was nice enough to count down the last minute, 10 seconds at a time, before he cranked up the volume. I loved baseball so much and was so happy to be covering a major league team in a pennant race that I wouldn't allow a creep like Miller or any of the other guys to ruin it for me.

The '79 series was also special for me because I got to spend two weeks working with Bob Prince, who had signed on with WTAE-TV to do pre- and postgame shows. Those were two of the most enjoyable weeks of my life.

The Pirates went back to Baltimore for Games 6 and 7, trailing three games to two. We were doing our editing for TV at WTAE's Hearst sister-station in Baltimore, WBAL. Nobody working there gave the Pirates a chance. How did I know that? When I walked into the station I noticed that every person in the newsroom was wearing a t-shirt and a hat that said "Baltimore Orioles 1979 World Champs."

This is strange, but something that sticks out in my mind as much as anything that happened in the games was a Secret Service agent. He was there to protect President Jimmy Carter, who had decided to show up for the game. The guy was sitting about three rows behind the third base dugout with his back to the field. The seat had actually been changed to face the wrong way.

My "press box" for the game was a seat at the back of the field-level section behind home plate. I watched this guy throughout the game and I can tell you that taxpayers got their money's worth out of him. He never once turned around to look at what was happening on the field. I always wondered if he was a sports fan or if they found somebody who didn't care about sports because, if he was a sports fan, that was one tough assignment.

Imagine the discipline it takes to sit three rows from the field for the seventh game of the World Series without ever laying your eyes on the field. He should have been given some kind of a medal.

3 – RENDEZ-VOUS '87

There aren't too many nice things you can say about the USSR, but they sure could make a sporting event interesting. The Summer and Winter Olympics are about 20 percent as compelling now as they were when the Big Bad Russians were using them to spread communist propaganda.

Back in 1987, the NHL put on what may have been the last meaningful all-star game in North America. It was the NHL All-Stars against the Soviet National Team, in Quebec City, Quebec. Mario Lemieux was in his third season with the Penguins and because at the time KDKA was the only Pittsburgh station covering him and the Penguins the way they deserved to be covered, I was there. (We were actually criticized by some sports columnists for spending too much time covering the Penguins. I had decided that Lemieux was the hockey equivalent of Babe Ruth and that he couldn't be over-covered.)

Boy, am I glad we went.

We stayed at the NHL hotel, the Hotel Frontenac, a turn-of-the-19th-century castle that's perched on a cliff overlooking the St. Lawrence Seaway, and the place was packed with media from all over the world. Rendez-vous '87 was a major international event. I even saw Wilt Chamberlin wandering around in the lobby.

I learned the real meaning of cold while I was there. The wind-chill factor was minus-60. I can remember getting out of the car and sprinting to the front door of the hotel. Two seconds in that air and it felt like someone was holding a lighted match to the end of your nose. No school cancellations, though. I remember seeing a school bus emptying a bunch of grade school kids out at a city park. They were there for a field trip to see the giant ice sculptures that, along with Rendez-vous '87, were part of the annual Winterfest celebration.

The Russians were still playing the game that the NHL, with Wayne Gretzky and the Edmonton Oilers, was just getting around to playing. Fast skaters going north and south. Watching them practice was awe-inspiring. Added to the great hockey atmosphere was the element that the Soviets always brought — international intrigue. While the Russian team practiced, mean-looking KGB agents were stationed all around the practice facility. I never saw one of them smile. They were there just in case one of the Russian players got crazy and decided to defect.

The huge Soviet Army choir was there, in uniform, to sing the Soviet National Anthem before the game. I'm not sure of the name of the song, but I think it was "We've Got Our Eye On You." Something like that.

It was quite a spectacle.

It was a two-game series and the NHL won the first one, 4-3, with

Lemieux assisting on the winning goal. The USSR won the second one, 5-3.

One last memory from one of the best events I ever covered: Boy, did the Soviet locker room stink. I was warned about it but I wasn't ready for the stench that hit me in the face when I walked in there and saw the uniforms hanging in their lockers. Maybe there was a shortage of laundry detergent in Mother Russia, but the hockey team was known worldwide for not washing their uniforms after games.

4 — VISITING ROBERTO CLEMENTE'S HOME

This was another one of those stories that made me really feel fortunate to be working in my hometown. I started watching Roberto Clemente play for the Pirates when I was 7 years old and he played in Pittsburgh for 18 years, so he was a major part of my life growing up. In 1987, I was producing stories for the Pirates TV pregame shows on KDKA called "Pirates Treasures." I did stories on Bill Mazeroski, Dale Long and Clemente. I spent time in the homes of both Maz and Long and did in-depth interviews with them. You know why Maz was important. Long was a big deal to me because I remembered when he set a record for hitting home runs in eight consecutive games in 1956. The Pirates were terrible in those days and Long's streak put them on the baseball map and had everybody in Pittsburgh and all over Major League Baseball talking about them. Clemente had been dead for 15 years and I had missed being able to cover him by one year. The first press pass that I had for a Pirates game was for the 1973 home opener when his number was retired.

When I was a kid, I know I never dreamed that someday I would be sitting in Roberto Clemente's living room in San Juan, Puerto Rico, but there I was and his wife, Vera, told me that nothing in the house had been changed since he had died on New Year's Eve 1972. Same furniture. Same carpeting (which was showing some fraying), same pictures on the wall, including a large, framed picture of Roberto wearing his double-knit Pirates jersey and the same knick-knacks on the tables.

She also showed me some of Roberto's paintings.

I wish I had known then that I would be writing a book because I would have made a much more detailed checklist of everything I saw there.

But it was just as much about how and where I saw so many interesting things as it was about what I saw.

After I did a long sit-down interview with Vera, she took me and the camera man, Richard Sutphen, down to the basement to see some of Roberto's trophies, awards and other possessions.

Picture being in your next-door neighbor's basement and he's showing you his youth baseball and bowling trophies and maybe his first baseball glove.

That's how it was for me, except that Vera was picking up silver bats that Roberto had won for winning batting titles and gold gloves that were as tarnished as your next door neighbor's bowling trophy. Everything was in a bin in an unorganized pile.

The plan, at the time, was to transfer all of the material to the Roberto Clemente Museum that was in the planning stages and would be located at Clemente's Sports City in San Juan.

I also paid a visit to Clemente's grade school and talked to his second grade teacher and I did a standup report in the field where he learned to play baseball.

The last standup I did was on the beach near the spot where his plane went down and I remember what I said to close out the story: "And of all the beautiful things that were said about Clemente in the days after his death, to me, the most powerful message was the one that came from the ALCOA sign high up on Mt. Washington and it was only two words. For several days, it flashed in big, red letters, "Adios Amigo.""

LEAST FAVORITE ASSIGNMENT

I — SUPER BOWL XL

It's finally Super Bowl Sunday and I'm sitting in my press box seat high above Ford Field in Detroit. Andrew Stockey, former sportscaster turned news anchor for WTAE-TV, arrives at the seat next to mine and emphatically puts his brief case on the counter and says, "This has been the worst week of my life."

Andrew was not the type to complain and, in fact, always seemed more enthusiastic about his job than most of the other guys in the Pittsburgh media who may have been around too long.

I knew exactly what he was talking about because I was right there with him. It was when I finally realized that it was time to find something else to do. The NFL was stupid to schedule the Super Bowl in Detroit. That goes without saying, but it was about a lot more than the cold, miserable weather. If you remember, the Steelers played all of their post-season games on the road that season. That meant that I was on the road from Tuesday through Sunday for three consecutive weeks. Unlike being on the road covering the Stanley Cup playoffs, there were no games to cover. No practices either, since you weren't given access to the field. It was three consecutive weeks of getting locker room sound bites and going to press conferences.

Excruciatingly boring.

Don't get me wrong. I always kept in mind that I was being paid well by KDKA to do something that most people would give anything to do and I always realized that even the worst assignment was better than sitting in a cubicle somewhere or digging a ditch.

I'll let you in on a secret. There were lots and lots of people in the Pittsburgh media who wouldn't have been upset if the Steelers had lost in the playoffs. They wanted their lives back. I know I sure did. We had our satellite truck set up in a parking lot outside Ford Field along with trucks from several other stations. We would fight city traffic every day to get to the press conferences to listen to players and coaches say the same things that they said yesterday and the day before that and the day before that. Then we would fight city traffic to get back to the satellite truck so that we could cram ourselves in the back and edit our reports. When it was time to go on the air, we would climb up on to some scaffolding that was situated so that a sign that read "Ford Field" could be seen behind us. WTAE was smart enough to set up in the lobby of the Steelers' hotel. Our field producer had us standing outside in the cold so that the viewers could barely see that we were standing in front of the stadium where the Super Bowl would be played.

You would do your two- or three-minute standup and then go into a warming truck and sit there for an hour waiting to do your next boring report. Working at KDKA had been on my nerves long before this trip, but this was the one that had me counting the days until I got out of there. Every day, I would have to speak to one of the four or five mid-20s-to early-30-something female producers back in KDKA's newsroom to find out what stories I should do. I had awards for reporting stuffed in desk drawers that were older than these people and I had to consult with them before deciding what story to do?

Someone had set up an interview with Jerome Bettis' high school football coach, so I went to his home in Detroit to do it. Bettis was the big story of that Super Bowl because he was a Detroit kid playing in the last game of his career. The interview went well and the cameraman got some good video of some still photographs that Bettis' coach had supplied to us. When I got back to our compound and prepared to write and edit the piece, the news producer called from Pittsburgh. She told me to give the tape to Ken Rice, who was co-anchoring our newscasts from Detroit with Patrice King Brown, so that Ken could write and front the story.

That's the kind of stuff that has sportscasters all over the country rooting for their local teams to lose — producers who know nothing about sports taking over the coverage of teams when they're playing their biggest games. It stinks. It's stupid and it's why I tell young guys who ask me for career advice to stay away from local news and get into radio.

The only way I could have enjoyed covering Super Bowl XL is if I had been able to parachute into Ford Field about 10 minutes before kickoff and just watch the game.

CHAPTER 39

LAST STOP
THE WRONG SIDE
OF THE MICROPHONE

OK, I confess. I was on the wrong side of the microphone for almost all of my 37 years as a sportscaster.

I was 25 when I got the job doing play-by-play of the Wichita Aeros, the Cubs' Triple "A" affiliate. Most of the players on that team were within a few years of my age.

Believe me, I would have preferred chasing balls in "AAA" outfields to chasing those guys around for interviews. As it turned out, I had a much better career than most of the guys that I interviewed in my three seasons as a play-by-play guy. I made it to the big leagues. Most of them never went beyond "AAA." I still would have rather been playing the games instead of announcing them.

I was hired to be KQV Radio's sports director in August of 1977, just as Terry Bradshaw was about to turn 29. I would be 29 that October. So, there I was, still covering guys who were my age. There were a few guys on the Steelers who were older than I, and a few of the stars were a few years younger, but, again, I would have rather been throwing passes like Bradshaw than throwing questions at him and his teammates in the locker room after games.

That's not to say that I would trade my life for any of the lives of the guys I covered. It's just that, at the time, I would have traded my job for theirs in a New York minute.

I always was aware that my job was a lot easier than theirs. They were the ones who faced the real pressure and had to perform. I was the guy who couldn't do what they did if my life depended on it.

That's why I think I always had more patience for their impatience with the media than a lot of my peers. I always realized how ridiculous it must have been for them to go out and perform at the highest level of their profession, as one of the best in the world at what they do, and then have to watch a scrawny weasel like me pick apart their performance.

I have a tremendous amount of respect for the doers.

I had a lot of unpleasant moments with Bill Cohwer and I was no fan of his. I thought he was a disaster and a jagoff at his Tuesday press conferences. That's why I stopped asking questions five or six years before he left. But, as much as I criticized him, I always knew that he was a doer and I was a guy who got paid for second-guessing and critiquing him, even though I couldn't be a good Pop Warner football coach, much less win a Super Bowl as an NFL head coach.

I don't expect any of the people I critiqued in my 37 years to waste their time reading this book, but if you run into any of them or if you know a current, big-time sports figure, do me a favor and give them a message.

Tell them that they exist so that idiots like me can critique and even ridicule them. They exist so that the poor slobs who work at jobs that they hate can have something to talk about around the coffee machine in the morning. Tell them that they get paid the big bucks because their job is to take regular human beings' minds off the stuff that really matters. Remind them that what they do doesn't really matter at all.

And remind them that what they and guys like me have to realize is that what we do sure beats having a real job.

ACKNOWLEDGEMENTS

THIS book could not have been written without the help of the real writer in the family, my brother Bill. Thanks also to Jim Wexell, author of "Steeler Nation," for his advice and encouragement.